ATLAS SHRUGGED:

Manifesto of the Mind

TWAYNE'S MASTERWORK STUDIES

Robert Lecker, General Editor

ATLAS SHRUGGED:

Manifesto of the Mind

Mimi Reisel Gladstein

TWAYNE PUBLISHERS
New York

PS
3535
.A547
A9435
2000
C. 2

Twayne's Masterwork Studies No. 174

Atlas Shrugged: *Manifesto of the Mind*
Mimi Reisel Gladstein

Twayne Publishers
1633 Broadway
New York, NY 10019

Library of Congress Cataloging-in-Publication Data
Gladstein, Mimi Reisel.
    Atlas shrugged : manifesto of the mind / Mimi Reisel Gladstein.
        p. cm. -- (Twayne's masterwork studies ; no. 174)
    Includes bibliographical references and index.
    ISBN 0-8057-1638- 6 (alk. paper)
    1. Rand, Ayn. Atlas shrugged. 2. Philosophy in literature. 3. Objectivism (Philosophy).
I. Title. II. Series
    PS3535.A547 A9435 2000
    813'.52--dc21   00-026894

This paper meets the requirements of ANSI/NISO Z3948-1992 (Permanence of Paper).

10 9 8 7 6 5 4 3 2

Printed in the United States of America

For Clifford and Alfred, Denise, Emilia,
and Lyla, my dividends

"Parentage is a very important profession,
but no test of fitness for it is ever imposed."
—*George Bernard Shaw*

Ayn Rand
CORBIS/Bettman

Contents

Note on the References and Acknowledgments

The most accessible edition of *Atlas Shrugged* in terms of both price and portability is the Signet paperback 35th anniversary edition. Although it is highly unusual to cite a paperback for this kind of scholarly study, taking into account the primary audiences for this book, I have chosen to do so. All parenthetical page references to the novel are to this edition.

One other primary text and two biographical works figure significantly in my reading of Rand and her most important novel. In the first place there are her notes to herself as she was writing, collected in *Journals of Ayn Rand*, edited by David Harriman, published in 1997 by Dutton. This work will be cited in the text as *J*. The only full-length biography published thus far is *The Passion of Ayn Rand*, written by Barbara Branden, who was an intimate of Rand's during the years that encompassed most of the writing, publication, and aftermath of *Atlas Shrugged*. References to Branden's biography will be made in the text and identified as *PAR*. Nathaniel Branden's memoir of his relationship with Rand, *My Years with Ayn Rand*, will be cited in the text as *MYWAR*.

Inevitably, some of the ideas in this study come from my previous works, in particular *The Ayn Rand Companion* (1984) and *The New Ayn Rand Companion, Revised and Updated* (1999), both published by Greenwood Press in Westport, Connecticut.

Special thanks are due to Chris Sciabarra, unfailingly generous and supportive as both critic and colleague, for reading an early draft of this manuscript and making many helpful suggestions. My thanks also to Bryan Register for his many constructive comments. Further acknowledgment of his contributions is made in the text. Finally, appreciation is due to David M. Brown for his insightful reading and commentary and timely turnaround during a busy season. Consultation with Douglas Den Uyl, as he prepared his volume on *The Fountainhead,* greatly facilitated my work. I am obliged to him, also, for sharing his prepublication manuscript.

Robert Lecker, the general editor of this series, wrote and invited me to prepare this volume. I am indebted to him for igniting the project and for his confidence in the finished product. Michelle Kovacs, at Twayne, was a pleasure to work with throughout. Appreciation is also due to the staff at Impressions, and to Anne Davidson at Twayne.

As always, I must acknowledge the love and encouragement of my husband, Jay, throughout this and every project. Though he may sometimes question the wisdom of the number of projects I undertake, his support has never wavered.

To all I owe thanks for any improvements their advice added to the text. However, in the end, a book such as this, particularly in the part that conveys interpretation and analysis of a work of fiction, is based on the reading of the author. While acknowledging the validity of alternative interpretations, the readings herein are based on my interpretations as a literary critic of *Atlas Shrugged,* speaking only for myself.

Chronology: Ayn Rand's Life and Works

1905	Alisa Zinovievna Rosenbaum born on February 2 in St. Petersburg, Russia. Her father was Zinovy Zacharovich Rosenbaum, and her mother Anna Borisovna Rosenbaum. Alisa was the eldest of three sisters. Her sisters were Natasha and Nora.
1914	Family travels to Austria, Switzerland, and England. Alisa decides she wants to become a writer. She reads "The Mysterious Valley," by Maurice Champagne, and falls in love with its hero, Cyrus. The heroine of her first novel bears the female equivalent of his name, Kira.
1914	Russia is at war with Germany and Austria (World War I).
1917–1918	Alisa witnesses first the Kerensky "Bloodless Revolution" and then the bloody "Bolshevik" revolution.
1918	Family leaves Petrograd and moves to Crimea. Alisa discovers the writings of Victor Hugo.
1921	Alisa graduates from gymnasium. Family returns to Petrograd, and she enters the University of Petrograd. She majors in history.
1924	Graduates from newly renamed University of Leningrad. Enrolls in State Institute for Cinematography.
1925	Publication date for *Pola Negri*, published in Moscow and Leningrad.
1926	Alisa Rosenbaum leaves for the United States. Lives with Portnoy relatives in Chicago. Adopts the name of Ayn Rand. Moves to Los Angeles. Meets Cecil B. DeMille, who gives her a job as an extra in *King of Kings*. Meets Frank O'Connor. *Hollywood: American City of Movies* published in Russia without Rand's knowledge.
1929	Marries Frank O'Connor.
1931	Becomes naturalized U.S. citizen.

1932	Original screenplay *Red Pawn* sold to Universal Studios, then purchased by Paramount, but never produced. Writes *Penthouse Legend.*
1933	Writing *We the Living;* sells *Penthouse Legend* to MGM.
1934	*Penthouse Legend* produced as *Woman on Trial* at Hollywood Playhouse. Writes *Ideal,* a play that was not produced in her lifetime. Sells *Penthouse Legend* for Broadway production and moves to New York City.
1935	*Night of January 16th* (Broadway title of *Penthouse Legend*) opens. Has six-month run.
1936	*We the Living* published by Macmillan.
1937	Writes *Anthem* but is unable to sell it. Works in the office of architect Ely Jacques Kahn to do research for *The Fountainhead.*
1938	*Anthem* published in England.
1939	Works on script for *The Unconquered,* play version of *We the Living,* produced by George Abbott.
1940	*The Unconquered* has unsuccessful five-day run on Broadway. Works on Wendell Willkie presidential campaign and meets some important "conservative" thinkers: Ruth Alexander, Albert Jay Nock, Rose Wilder Lane, and Isabel Paterson.
1941	Signs contract with Bobbs-Merrill to publish *The Fountainhead.*
1942	Finishes *The Fountainhead.*
1943	*The Fountainhead* published in May. Sells movie rights to Warner Brothers and returns to live in California to write the screenplay.
1944	Becomes screenwriter for Hal Wallis; writes screenplay for *Love Letters.* Buys home in Tarzana designed by Richard Neutra.
1945	*Anthem* published in first U.S. edition by Pamphleteers.
1946	Begins writing *The Strike,* working title for *Atlas Shrugged.*
1947	Testifies before House Un-American Activities Committee. Writes "Screen Guide for Americans," published in *Plain Talk.*
1949	*The Fountainhead* film version is released.
1950	Meets fans Nathan Blumenthal, later Nathaniel Branden, and Barbara Weidman, later Barbara Branden. Significant relationship begins.
1951	Moves back to New York City to work full-time on *Atlas Shrugged.*
1957	*Atlas Shrugged* published.
1958	Nathaniel Branden Institute (NBI) begins teaching Ayn Rand's philosophy. She helps write "Basic Principles of Objectivism."

Chronology

1960	Speaks at Yale University.
1961	*For the New Intellectual* published. Delivers first of Ford Hall Forum lectures in Boston.
1962	Starts *The Objectivist Newsletter,* coedited with Nathaniel Branden. *Who Is Ayn Rand?* by Nathaniel Branden and Barbara Branden published. First book about her and her work.
1963	Awarded doctor of humane letters, honorary degree, by Lewis and Clark College.
1964	*The Virtue of Selfishness* published. *Playboy* interview published in March.
1966	*Capitalism: The Unknown Ideal* published. *The Objectivist* replaces *The Objectivist Newsletter.*
1968	Nathaniel Branden Institute closes.
1971	*The Romantic Manifesto* published. *The New Left: The Anti-industrial Revolution* published. *The Ayn Rand Letter* begins publication after *The Objectivist* stops.
1974	"Philosophy: Who Needs It" lecture delivered to West Point graduating class.
1976	January–February is last issue of *The Ayn Rand Letter.*
1979	*Introduction to Objectivist Epistemology* published. Frank O'Connor dies.
1981	"Sanction of the Victims," last public speech, delivered at the annual conference of the National Committee for Monetary Reform in New Orleans.
1982	Ayn Rand dies on March 6. *Philosophy: Who Needs It* published posthumously.

LITERARY AND
HISTORICAL CONTEXT

1

Rand's World: Global and Personal

The Russian world that awaited the birth of Alisa Zinovievna Rosenbaum on February 2, 1905, was a world in the throes of impending cataclysm. War and revolution were the background and the foreground. The Russo-Japanese War was in progress, culminating in the destruction of the Baltic fleet in the Straits of Tsushima in May 1905. That year also saw a revolution that set up the first of a number of Dumas, elected legislatures that held the promise of more political and civil liberties than the people had experienced under the autocratic rule of the czars. Dumas were elected and dissolved; Stolypin, the prime minister during the second and third Dumas, was murdered, as was the self-styled "holy monk" Rasputin, who held the czarina under his sway. Before Alisa's teenage years, the Russian army, without popular support and sufficient supplies, suffered massive casualties and retreats in World War I. St. Petersburg, the beautiful imperial city of Alisa's birth, became Petrograd, the cradle of revolution. The Romanov dynasty ended, and the Union of Soviet Socialist Republics was born. There could not have been a world more unsuited to a woman whose "theme song" rang with individualism. In her own words: "Call it fate or irony, but I was born, of all countries on earth in the one [least] suitable for a fanatic of individualism: Russia."[1]

3

The eldest of three daughters of Zinovy Zacharovich and Anna Borisovna Rosenbaum, Alisa was recognized in early childhood for the quality of her mind. She was raised in relative comfort, what might even appear as luxury in a contemporary context. Cooks, governesses, nurses, and maids were part of the family retinue. Trips to Crimean resorts and lengthy summer sojourns in Austria and Switzerland were also part of Alisa's childhood memories.[2] It was in London, while walking with her governess, that Alisa first realized that she wanted to become a writer, and though she was not mature enough at that point to articulate it, her tastes went strongly toward the romantic.

That is apt, for Ayn Rand's life was in many ways every bit as romantic as her fiction. She overcame great adversity to become a best-selling author and leader of an intellectual movement. She attracted devoted fans; she provoked vicious detractors. Her death did little to change that. Although she has gained certain legitimacy in academe—the American Philosophical Association now has an Ayn Rand Society—she still provokes marked hostility in many quarters. Her cultural and intellectual impact has grown, and there are more Objectivist organizations and publications now than there were in her lifetime. But although the interest in, and adherence to, her ideas has grown, the animosities and schisms created by her opinions have also outlived her. A 1998 article in *U.S. News and World Report* details the conflicts of what the author, Marci McDonald, calls "Fighting over Ayn Rand." A passionate intensity defines the quality of her life, as outlined in the appropriately titled biography *The Passion of Ayn Rand,* by Barbara Branden.

Rand's passions were inspired early and lasted throughout her lifetime. During one summer trip to the Crimea, little Alisa first heard the light classics and popular music pieces, liltingly joyous, that she named her "tiddlywink" music. It was the same music that would be played at her funeral. In the Crimea, she saw a young English girl, playing tennis, who came to represent for Rand the symbol of the independent foreign woman, long legged and agile. Rand evoked that image for her ideal heroine, Dagny Taggart, in a scene that highlighted those long legs and tennis-playing ability.

The last idyllic trip the Rosenbaums took as a family was to Vienna for a week, followed by six weeks in Switzerland, where Alisa enjoyed climbing in the mountains. The vacation ended with the outbreak of World War I and the family's hurried trip to London to catch a ship for a dangerous voyage back to Russia.

Much of the drama and trauma that accompanied the end of the Romanov dynasty and the birth of the Union of Soviet Socialist Republics took place, figuratively speaking, on the Rosenbaum family's doorstep. There were strikes, crime was rampant, and food was in short supply. When she was 12 years old, Alisa saw the National Guard fire on an anti-czarist crowd. However, the next day, the soldiers refused to fire and joined the revolution. That revolution culminated in the selection of Alexander Kerensky, one of Alisa's first real-life heroes, as prime minister.

Even in her youth, Alisa assumed the importance of a moral basis for politics. Particularly she concluded that individual freedom had to be the basis for any moral system of government, and she believed that Kerensky was fighting for just such a system. It was not to be. The return to Russia of the Bolshevik revolutionaries, among them Lenin, Stalin, Molotov, and Trotsky, doomed the new government. As the situation deteriorated, the Bolsheviks made their move. In the "ten days that shook the world," they captured Petrograd, arrested the Kerensky cabinet, and murdered delegates to the Constitutional Assembly. Alisa witnessed the funeral procession from her balcony.

Kerensky was able to flee the country, but the Rosenbaum family did not. Alisa's father felt he could not leave his business. But soon there was no business to leave; it was confiscated by the state. The family fortunes took a decided turn for the worse.

From the outset, Alisa reacted against what she considered to be the immoral basis of communism. For her, it was a sacrifice of the good and the best to the mediocre and the commonplace. In her reaction to the horror of communism was born a theme that would echo in all her writing. That theme is the fundamental and paramount human right of a person to his or her own life. No group, be it family, community, country, or larger entity, has a claim on that. In years to come, many leftists or communist sympathizers would argue that the ideals of communism were good, but that they had not really been put into practice anywhere. The writer that Alisa became illustrated in her fiction and explained in her nonfiction why communism was at base an immoral system, a system rooted in faulty premises.

From 1921 to 1924, Alisa attended the University of Petrograd, renamed for Lenin in the last year of her studies. She majored in history and minored in philosophy. Her father was not happy with her choice of subject matter, wanting her to learn a profession. Because she was an avid fan of the American cinema, after graduation, she enrolled in the State Institute for Cinematography. Two studies that she wrote about film, *Pola Negri* (about the actress by that name) and *Hollywood: American City of Movies,* were published in Russian without her knowledge. She learned about them from her mother, who wrote her about seeing the booklets in a store window, after Alisa was already in the United States. In 1999 the Ayn Rand Institute republished facsimiles and translations of these booklets, along with some other notations Rand had made about movies and movie stars, under the title *Ayn Rand: Russian Writings on Hollywood.*

Her university years were a time of great struggle and change within the country. The Union of Soviet Socialist Republics was established in 1922, and a battle ensued for the leadership of the country. Stalin eventually succeeded Lenin. His reign was one of the longest and bloodiest in history. By most accounts, he is responsible for more deaths than Hitler. Stalin created the so-called Iron Curtain, designed both to keep foreign influences and people out and to keep Russian citizens in. Once it had descended, few were able to get out of Russia. It was only a fortuitous set of circumstances that resulted in Alisa's securing a visa to visit relatives in the United States. Her mother sold the last of her jewelry to help finance the passage. Although the trip was ostensibly for a "visit," Alisa never planned to return.

In any time period, it takes considerable courage to travel halfway around the world to live by yourself in a country where you don't speak the language fluently. In the early part of this century, such a move was a momentous step for a young woman. Women had only recently acquired the right to vote in the United States, and the United States was considered one of the most advanced countries in the world in the area of women's rights.

Alisa's first stop was Riga, Latvia, where she saw five films. She then went on to Berlin, where she visited a cousin who had left Russia a few months earlier. From Berlin Alisa went first to Paris and then to Le Havre, where she boarded a ship for the long trip across the Atlantic. During this trip, as she made her way from the Old World to the new, she turned 21; she also adopted a new name, Ayn, a name of Finnish origin. There has been some speculation about the genesis of her chosen nom de plume. An explanation with some currency, supported by a cousin's recollection of the incident, is that Alisa took the name "Rand" from the Remington-Rand typewriter that she brought with her from Russia. In a May 1997 story in *Impact,* the newsletter of the Ayn Rand Institute, there is reference to archival materials that suggest that Alisa Rosenbaum had selected her professional name before she left Russia. The article cites letters from family in Russia that refer to the name "Rand" before Alisa wrote from America. The article also cites a *New York Evening Post* story in which Rand reveals that fact. A 1926 letter from her sister Nora has clever drawings of the name "Ayn Rand" up in "lights." When the Cyrillic spelling of her name is studied, one finds resemblances to both the names "Ayn" and "Rand."

In contrast to the country she left, the United States that welcomed Rand was experiencing a time of prosperity and frivolity that F. Scott Fitzgerald would name the Jazz Age. Rand noted in a letter to a friend in Russia that Americans never take anything too seriously; they are always joking and wisecracking. She delighted in the general cheerful tone of the times, especially coming from the gray dreariness of the Soviet Union. Even the Maxwell House coffee "good to the last drop" animated sign on Broadway thrilled her. New York City left an indelible impression on her, and it would always be her favorite place. The New York skyline embodied for her, in concrete and glass form, the concept of the soaring heights of human potential.

Her Chicago stay with relatives was brief. Chicago was not a city she cared for. This is curious, since an important character in her breakthrough novel *The Fountainhead* is modeled on Louis Sullivan, a pioneer of modern skyscraper design, whose architectural creations are significant in the Chicago cityscape. Her family provided a letter of recommendation to the DeMille Studios for a job as a junior screenwriter. As soon as it was feasible, Rand set off to fulfill her goal of becoming a screenwriter for the movies, but when she got there she was told there were no jobs available. Then, in a turn of events that one could describe as "just like in the movies," she met DeMille, who took an instant liking to her. DeMille showed her around the studio so that she could see how movies were made; then he gave her jobs, first as an extra in *King of Kings,* then as a junior screenwriter. His nickname for her was "Caviar." It was on the set of *King of Kings* that she saw the man she would marry, Frank O'Connor.

Although Rand often wrote about falling in love with him at first sight, of his good looks and aristocratic bearing, and of how Frank fit her image of the ideal man, there is little information about his feelings about their meeting and relationship. The actual marriage, some three years later in April 1929, seems to have been precipitated by the impending expiration of Rand's visa, as noted both in Branden's biography and in *Ayn Rand: A Sense of Life,* the documentary film about her life. Frank and his brother Nick joked about which one of them would have to marry her to keep her from being deported. Once Frank and Ayn were married, the couple had to go to Mexico so that she could reenter the United States legally as the wife of a citizen. Rand received her citizenship papers in March 1931. The marriage was to last 50 years.

The tenor of the times changed dramatically shortly after the marriage. The stock market crash in October 1929 led to the years of the Great Depression, a time of drastically reduced economic expectations. Large numbers of people were out of work. The young couple had many years of struggle. At the time of her marriage, Ayn Rand listed "waiter" as her occupation. In the hard times that followed, Rand worked in the wardrobe department of RKO, eventually rising to head of the department. It was not work she enjoyed.

The 1930s brought a whole new ethos. Gone were the gay and devil-may-care times of the previous decade. The population became more receptive to government intervention in what had heretofore been private matters. This was not solely a matter of response to the depression.

The early part of the twentieth century found the world awash with collectivist-inspired political movements and theories, to which many artists and intellectuals were attracted. Most of these theories and movements fit under the general category of socialism, to use a term that broadly denotes a system of public, as opposed to private, ownership and management of the means of production and distribution of goods. And the varieties of statism were many, from the moderate evolutionary Fabian Society of England to the militant National Socialist German Workers' party of Hitler.

The Communist Manifesto is perhaps the most celebrated of socialist documents, and Marxian socialism spread throughout Europe in the late nineteenth and early twentieth centuries. In fact, socialist parties developed in all the leading industrial nations. In Russia there were four kinds of socialist parties; it was the Bolsheviks who prevailed. In China, Sun Yat-sen had led a socialist revolution as early as 1912. The Russian Revolution led to a Leninist interpretation of Marx called communism, a term generally associated with the ideas and practices of the Russian Marxists, particularly those who became the developers of the Soviet system of government. For many young intellectuals and artists worldwide, the Russian Revolution was a noble experiment. They excused the poor standard of living and lack of freedom in the Soviet Union as transitional necessities. Socialism was in such ascendance during this time that the 1930s are sometimes called "the Red Decade."

One of the reasons that it is difficult to accurately define socialism is that it has taken different forms under different historical and local conditions. Part of its appeal is that it is advanced as a movement for the promotion of the well-being and happiness of individual men and women, the greatest happiness of the greatest number. In its design, the state is supposed to exist only as a means to that end and then, theoretically, is supposed to wither away. In practice, the opposite has been true. Whenever and wherever socialist-based governments have been set up, the state and its apparatus have grown exponentially. Collectivist-inspired movements in the Soviet Union, Nazi Germany, and Communist China have resulted in totalitarian states.

Ayn Rand, unlike the majority of her peers who were beguiled by the promise of collectivism, was writing antisocialist fiction. Ever the individualist, she set herself against the zeitgeist. Her first novels, *We the Living* and *Anthem,* expose the flaws of both the system and the philosophy underlying the communist state and collectivist mentality. In *We the Living,* she writes from personal experience about how communism destroys individual happiness, particularly in the best and the brightest. In *Anthem* she illustrates how a "We" based society kills invention, creativity, and production. Not unexpectedly, she had difficulty getting an American publisher for *Anthem.* It was published first in England, and it was not until Rand had made her name as the best-selling author of *The Fountainhead* that *Anthem* found an American publisher.

Contiguous with writing *We the Living,* Rand also wrote a play inspired by her reading of the Ivar Kreugar debacle. Ivar Kreugar was an immigrant who came to this country with little money, built an international financial empire, and controlled half the world's match industry. When the bogus basis for his company was discovered, he committed suicide. Rand's title for the play, which created the novel dramatic device of having each performance's audience serve as a jury, was *Penthouse Legend.* When the play was originally produced in Hollywood, the title was changed to *Woman on Trial.* Its absent hero, Bjorn Faulkner, is clearly a criminal in realistic terms, but as Rand later made clear, the events of the play are not to be taken literally, for the play is a work of romantic symbolism. She called it a "sense of life" play. The name was changed to *Night of January 16th* when the work was moved to Broadway, where it enjoyed a moderate success. Rand and her husband moved to New York City to participate in the production of the play. It was a happy move, as Rand had always wanted to live in New York, a city that represented for her the essence of American aspiration and reality.

Unfortunately, the production of her first Broadway play did not turn out to be a positive experience. It was a pitched battle, which Rand later characterized as "hell." She quarreled constantly with the producer about changes he wanted her to make. Subsequently she sued him for withholding some of her royalties. Nevertheless, the play did enjoy moderate success and has, since its initial production, been remounted often by little theater and summer stock companies. It was even made into a movie starring Robert Preston and Ellen Drew, but the movie is very different from the play.

During this time Rand was also trying to get her family out of Russia. Telegrams during the mid-thirties show that at one point they expected permission to leave, but in the end, consent was not granted, and Rand had reason to believe that continued correspondence would put her family in jeopardy. She lost contact with them during World War II and many years later learned of the death of her father, mother, and sister Natasha during the German siege of Leningrad. In the 1970s, Rand was able to bring her youngest and favorite sister, Nora, to the United States, but the visit turned out to be a disaster, and Nora and her husband, Victor, returned to Soviet Russia.

Rand's anticommunist views and anticollectivist themes did not resonate with leading critics and publishers during the 1930s. There is also reason to believe that she had difficulties in finding jobs as a screenwriter because of her political stance. On the international stage, rumblings of war persisted. Events in the 1930s moved the world steadily and inexorably toward global war. Fascism, which had first gained power in Italy under Benito Mussolini, was victorious under Hitler in Germany. In the Far East, Japan exercised its aggressive and militaristic muscle and invaded Manchuria. The countries that made up what became the Allied powers did little to check aggression, and the invasions continued. Italy bombed Ethiopia; Germany marched into the Rhineland. In Spain, a civil war resulted in a victory for General Francisco Franco, whose forces were supplied and reinforced by both Germany and Italy in what many saw as a dress rehearsal for a major war. Austria capitulated, and Czechoslovakia fell before the Nazi juggernaut. In 1939, having signed a pact with Russia, Germany invaded Poland. Soviet forces also encroached on Polish territory, and the country was partitioned between Germany and Russia. Russia also invaded Finland.

There is not much in Ayn Rand's writing that addresses this run-up to World War II. Among her letters is one accompanying a contribution to the fund for purchasing armaments for Finland. Many left-leaning intellectuals were active in antifascist activity but supportive of Soviet Russia, which became an ally once Germany attacked it in 1941. Ayn Rand seems to have been one of the few who argued that there was little philosophical difference between fascism and communism. Both demand that the individual live for the state; both promote totalitarian states. When Dashiel Hammett sent her a ticket to an antifascist event, she returned it, writing him that when he opposed both communism and fascism, she would send him double the amount of the ticket. She wrote that capitalists must oppose both of these evil "isms."

During this time she wrote "The Individualist Manifesto," which in a greatly reduced version was published in *Reader's Digest* as "The Only Path to Tomorrow." Headlines trumpeted the fall of nations; slowly and inexorably, the war spread globally, but Rand's published letters and journal entries do not touch on war. She was to write that the only justified war was one of self-defense. Certainly much of World War II fell into that category. The United States did not join the war until it was attacked by the Japanese at Pearl Harbor, so U.S. involvement could be defined as falling into Rand's criteria for a just war.

Whether or not Rand's writing touched on World War II, Branden's biography notes what must have been her anguish as she read the news about the Russian front, in particular about the siege of Leningrad. Other accounts of Rand's life mention the war's effect on her mainly in terms of the quality of paper used in the publication of *The Fountainhead* and the publisher's concern, owing to paper shortages, about the book's length. One reviewer even made paper rationing an issue in her assessment of the book. Another direct effect was that rationing of certain materials delayed the production of the movie of the novel.

Rand and her husband moved back to California in 1943 to await the film version of her novel. She had done an initial treatment and hoped to be hired to write the final screenplay. When their cats could not be accommodated in rented apartments, they bought a beautiful home, originally owned by Josef von Sternberg, and designed by Richard Neutra. It was on a small ranch in the San Fernando Valley. Existent photographs of the place reveal lush grounds and a most attractive house, which were featured in a *House and Garden* article. Frank O'Connor was happy on the ranch, tending the grounds, raising flowers and peacocks. It all spoke to his strong artistic bent; he became a painter in later life. Ayn and Frank lived on the ranch until 1951, when Rand decided they needed to move back to New York City, where she lived for the rest of her life.

In California during the 1940s, the O'Connors made many new friends and entertained often in their new home. Frank Lloyd Wright, who had refused an interview before the publication of *The Fountainhead,* invited Ayn and Frank to visit him at Taliesin East, and they did. The result was a commission for him to design a home for them; the design was never built.

While awaiting the production of the film version of *The Fountainhead,* Rand took a job with Hal Wallis. The job called for her to work six months of the year writing for Wallis and to be free for her own writing the other six. Her professional assignments during this time produced two successful movie scripts. One was *Love Letters;* the other was *You Came Along.* Both were adaptations of other writers' works. Wallis also suggested that Rand write an original screenplay about the development of the atom bomb. The working title was "Top Secret," but before the script was finished, Wallis sold it to MGM, much to Rand's chagrin.

Following World War II, in which the United States and the Soviet Union had found themselves allies, relations between the two countries deteriorated. What followed came to be called the Cold War because the enmity between the Soviet Union and the countries under its influence and the rest of the Allied countries took every form except open warfare. In the United States, fear of communist infiltration and influence led to what is sometimes called the McCarthy era, a period of concern about communist infiltration of the government and investigation of communist influence in many sensitive areas.

In Hollywood, Rand had made many friends who were political conservatives and who shared some of her anticollectivist views. She wrote "Screen Guide for Americans" for the anticommunist Motion Picture Alliance for the Preservation of American Ideals. In it she exposed the methods of undermining American values in film and admonished moviemakers not to glorify failure or smear American political institutions, free enterprise, and industrialists. When the House Un-American Activities Committee held hearings about Hollywood, she testified, but she was not interested in addressing any issue but the one of ideology. She was not allowed to testify as she wanted, and the whole episode remained a source of discomfort for her. She did not think it was an issue for the government to handle. She later argued that much was known about the blacklisting of unfriendly witnesses, but little was known about how witnesses who were friendly to the purposes of the committee were also persecuted and maligned.

The movie version of *The Fountainhead* was not a resounding success. Critics panned it, and it did not fulfill Rand's original conception. It did, however, stimulate sales of the novel. Fans who had already read the novel anxiously awaited the film. Rand received and responded to numerous fan letters. Her habit of responding to fans led to a relationship that significantly affected the rest of her life. But before that happened, she had begun work on her next novel.

Not long after the publication of *The Fountainhead*, Rand was inspired by an idea that became the plot line for *Atlas Shrugged*. The story goes that during a telephone conversation with a friend, Rand was told that she had to write a full explication of her ideas in nonfiction treatise form, that she had a duty to do so. Rand questioned this definition of her "duty" and responded, "What if I went on strike? What if all creative minds in the world went on strike?" (*PAR*, 218). It immediately struck her that such an idea would be a good basis for a novel, but she did not begin making notes until 1945.[3] From its initial conception, her next work was to be a novel about the mind on strike, and "The Strike" remained its working title for almost a decade.

The film version of *The Fountainhead* came out in 1949. That same year, a young Canadian fan of the novel, who was studying at UCLA, wrote Ayn Rand a follow-up letter to one he had mailed earlier while still in Canada. In early 1950 the interchange resulted in an invitation to her home. Nathan Blumenthal (later Nathaniel Branden) describes the visit as "entering the dimension of my most passionate longing." The meeting between the 19-year-old student and the 45-

year-old author was charged with instant attraction. While Frank O'Connor listened and served refreshments, Ayn and Nathaniel conversed intently until early the next morning. Later Branden wrote that their love affair began with "discussions of epistemology, metaphysics, and ethics." The physical affair did not begin till some years later. Following the initial meeting, Nathaniel asked permission to bring a friend to a subsequent meeting. A week later, Barbara Weidman (later Barbara Branden) joined the discussions.

Both young students were captivated by Rand's extraordinary intellect. Nathaniel concluded that she was "more than anything I could have imagined." He called her "Mrs. Logic." Barbara remembers the "fiercely perceptive eyes" and the intellectual excitement of conversing with a woman who was "a superb teacher, taking endless joy in the activity of breaking down complex issues into their easily graspable parts" (*PAR*, 235). Barbara and Nathaniel, who Rand referred to as "the children," were involved in a troublesome relationship of their own. Both credit Rand with influencing them toward marriage. When they did marry in 1953, Ayn Rand and Frank O'Connor were their matron of honor and best man.

In 1951 Nathaniel and Barbara moved from California to New York City, she to begin her graduate work in philosophy, he to continue his undergraduate degree in psychology. Shortly afterward Ayn Rand and her husband also moved there. In New York, a group of friends and relatives of the Brandens began to meet regularly at Rand's apartment. Individually, they were drawn to Rand either because they had been admirers of *The Fountainhead* or because in the stimulation of interacting with Rand they became interested in her ideas. This group, which became part of her inner circle, expanded and shrunk over the years and was known variously as the "Class of '43" in acknowledgment of the publication date of *The Fountainhead* or "the Collective," an ironic self-description. The most durable member of the group was Leonard Peikoff, Barbara's cousin, who met Rand when he was 17 years old. Eventually, he became Rand's heir and literary executor and chairman emeritus of the Ayn Rand Institute. The most famous member of the group, in terms of global impact, was Alan Greenspan, who had been married briefly to Joan Mitchell, Barbara's dearest childhood friend. Greenspan, an economic consultant when he met Rand, went on to be an adviser to three presidents and eventually chairman of the Federal Reserve, shepherding the U.S. economy during a period of unprecedented prosperity. He remained a loyal friend of Rand's for the rest of her life, even inviting her to Washington, D.C., for his swearing in as part of the Gerald Ford administration.

As she worked through the final stages of writing *Atlas Shrugged,* Rand's social life was made up almost entirely of interaction with the Collective. Barbara and Nathaniel Branden had been accorded the privilege of reading early chapters of *Atlas Shrugged* while they were still in California. Once the small group of their friends and intimates began meeting for regular Saturday evening discussions with Rand, the group also became prepublication readers.

What members of the Collective did not realize, though they certainly knew that Nathaniel was Rand's favorite and designated ideal reader—the term she used to explain the dual dedication of *Atlas Shrugged* to him and her husband—was that what had begun as a mentor-fan relationship was expanding into a full-fledged love affair. The affair would have fateful consequences for all involved.[4] It began in early 1955 and progressed through periods of greater and lesser intensity, sometimes including a sexual component, sometimes not. It ended cataclysmically in 1968, rupturing family relationships and ending friendships, creating a schism in the adherents to Rand's philosophy that endures to this day. But before that fateful day, a philosophy was born and an intellectual movement launched.

In her personal life, Ayn Rand began an affair with a man 25 years her junior; in her professional life, she began writing the climax of her magnum opus, a 60-page speech delivered by her ideal man. The speech took two years to write. When the novel was finished in March 1957, Ayn Rand did not know that it was to be her last published work of fiction. Random House won the contest to publish the novel, and although Rand would not allow them to cut one word, they promoted the book aggressively. Rand even spoke to a meeting of Random House salespeople, consolidating her philosophy for them as follows: "Metaphysics—objective reality; Epistemology—reason; Ethics—self-interest; Politics—capitalism."[5]

Rand expected a fusillade of negative reactions to the novel because she understood that its message flew in the face of the predominant cultural tradition. Her expectations were fulfilled. Those reviews, the hostile and the sympathetic, are presented in some detail in chapter 2 of this volume. What Rand had not anticipated, and what her friends believe sent her into a deep depression, was the lack of support from people she counted on to share her philosophical perspectives. Readers, however, were undeterred. As was the case with *The Fountainhead,* word of mouth trumped negative criticism. *Atlas Shrugged* went through printing after printing and has never been out of print since it was published. After Rand's break with Nathaniel Branden, his name was removed from the dedication. In 1992 Leonard Peikoff published a 35th anniversary edition, with a new introduction. The novel has been translated into languages as diverse as Hebrew and Spanish.

Rand's career moved in an unexpected direction the year after the publication of *Atlas Shrugged.* Nathaniel Branden began to teach the basic principles of Rand's philosophy, which she named Objectivism. These lectures became incorporated under the Nathaniel Branden Institute (NBI), a business venture undertaken by the Brandens, approved by Rand. Nathaniel Branden explains that his motivation was his need to take action in the face of the animosity of the responses to the novel: "My motive was selfish—it was *my* battle for *my* ideas" (*MYWAR*, 206).

No one could have predicted the growth of what came to be called the Objectivist movement. Ayn Rand did not expect it to succeed when she agreed to be available for question-and-answer sessions after the lectures; the businesspeople Rand consulted saw no future for such an impractical venture. Starting in the winter of 1958 with a class of 28 students, the undertaking metamorphosed over the years to include courses in many cities, a newsletter called *The Objectivist Newsletter* and then the journal called *The Objectivist,* and the publication of Rand's many speeches and articles. Ayn Rand and Objectivist study clubs sprang up on college campuses. A publishing division was created to reissue some of Rand's favorite novels with new introductions by Rand. *Calumet "K"* and *The Man Who Laughs* were the first to be issued under the NBI imprint. Even art reproductions were added to the enterprise. In its heyday, NBI sponsored balls and baseball games, movies and fashion shows.

As Rand began to emerge from her post–*Atlas Shrugged* depression, her writing was inspired by the need for further elucidation of her ideas. *Atlas Shrugged* was the foundation, the dramatization, and the cornerstone for her subsequent career as a philosopher. Following the novel's publication and until her death, the elaboration of her ideas would be published in anthologies of collected essays, including several posthumous volumes. She never published another novel.

2

Critical Reception

The critical reception of *Atlas Shrugged* began even before the novel was published. This was due, in part, to the uncommon circumstances of its creation. On the one hand, there were the members of "the Class of '43," a nickname Ayn Rand gave to a group of young people, mostly friends and relatives of Nathaniel and Barbara Branden, who were fans of *The Fountainhead*, which had been published in 1943. This group of young intellectuals met regularly at Rand's home on Saturday nights, and they read *Atlas Shrugged* in manuscript even as it was being written. This is not a usual procedure. Because they were intensely partisan, it is not unexpected that they were uncritically positive about what they were reading. The more naive among them expected that it was a book that would be enthusiastically welcomed and effect immediate change in the country. One is reminded of Jonathan Swift's Lemuel Gulliver, who cannot understand why the publications of his *Travels* has produced so little reform in England: "Behold, after above six months warning, I cannot learn that my book hath produced one single effect according to mine intentions.... And, it must be owned that seven months were sufficient time to correct every vice and folly to which Yahoos are subject, if their natures had been capable of the least disposition to virtue and Wisdom."[6] Later, I will discuss other areas where Rand's fiction techniques have much in common with traditional satirists.

On the other hand, a group of editors and readers at key publishing houses were reading the book in a quasi contest to see who would gain the rights to publish it. It would have been expected that the publisher of Rand's previous novel, *The Fountainhead,* would have uncontested rights to publishing her next novel, but Rand had not been pleased with the way Bobbs-Merrill had fumbled both the publication and the promotion of *The Fountainhead.* Therefore, when Ross Baker, the New York representative of Bobbs-Merrill, suggested that she cut the length of one of the important philosophical speeches in *Atlas Shrugged,* Rand seized the opportunity to free herself from her contract. Because Bobbs-Merrill refused to publish the novel as she had written it, Rand felt she had complied with the need to give them right of first refusal and could seek another publisher. Baker's assessment was that the book was "unsalable and unpublishable" as written (*PAR,* 284).

Bennett Cerf, whose Random House won the opportunity to become the book's publisher, concluded, after his first reading: "It's a great book. Name your own terms" (*PAR,* 287). These two diametrically opposed prepublication evaluations of the book are paradigmatic of the critical reaction that was to follow. It is awful; it is great. The argument still rages.

Rand had premonitions that her novel would provoke negative reactions. She told Nathaniel Branden, "It's going to be the most controversial book of this century; I'm going to be hated, vilified, lied about, smeared in every possible way" (*MYWAR,* 176). She was close to being right. Hostile reviewers predominated. To add to the challenges the book had to overcome to reach its audience, acrimonious reviews were published in some of the most influential newspapers and magazines. Granville Hicks, writing in the *New York Times Book Review,* proclaims *Atlas Shrugged* a book "written out of hate" and uses such adjectives as "belligerent and unremitting" to describe its tone. He finds Rand's creation of a dark and devastated New York City an exercise in projected misanthropy, opining that she "cheerfully envisages" such a destruction.

"Liberals" are identified by Donald Malcolm, in his review for the *New Yorker*, as Rand's villains, and he finds her depiction of how they have brought "the world to a sorry plight" a strain on credulity. His derisive descriptions of the novel include the scene where the incompetent liberals attempt to torture John Galt ("no fooling, these liberals can't do anything right") and Dagny and Hank's viewing of a man pulling a plow by hand in Michigan ("Even the horse, it appears, cannot survive where liberals flourish and billboards disappear").

William F. Buckley's antipathy to Ayn Rand was unabated even by her death. His obituary notice is positively celebratory. It is not surprising, then, that the *National Review* assessment, written by reformed communist Whittaker Chambers, is among the most vitriolic. Adjectives such as "silly," "bumptious," and "preposterous" pepper the early part of his review, which characterizes the novel as a "ferroconcrete fairy tale," a modern day take on "The War between the Children of Light and the Children of Darkness." Finally, Chambers denounces the book for its "overriding arrogance," its "shrillness," and its "dogmatism." His most insulting assessment, given the author's Jewish background, is that "from almost any page of *Atlas Shrugged*, a voice can be heard ... commanding: 'To a gas chamber—go!' "

Reviewers seemed to fall over themselves in a contest to devise the most pejorative descriptors for the novel. "Execrable claptrap" and "solemn grotesquerie" are Charles Rolo's entries. His *Atlantic Monthly* review found that here and there Rand's "perceptions are sound," but that for the most part, the book, which he says exerted on him a "repulsive fascination," is an act of hatred. The *Time* evaluation begins, "Is it a novel? Is it a nightmare?" and goes on to announce that the novel must be read to be disbelieved. The *Time* reviewer found the book a "weird performance" and a hideous caricature of capitalism. *Catholic World*'s reviewer Riley Hughes adds "shrill diatribe" to the disparaging catalog of descriptions. Patricia Donegan accuses Rand of "gleefully destroy[ing] the world" and of expressing "an immense hostility, a real malevolence that takes joy in the sight of destruction." For Donegan, the novel is an "outpouring of hate." One can add to the foregoing the *Los Angeles Times'* "grotesque eccentricity" and Gore Vidal's "perfect in its immorality."

The extreme denunciations were not matched by an equal number of raves in favor of the work, but there were some reviewers who found much to admire about the novel. Chief among them was John Chamberlain writing for the *New York Herald Tribune*. Chamberlain discerned the various levels of the novel and understood its ability to "satisfy many readers on many separate planes of satisfaction." He compares it to Buck Rogers as science fiction and Dostoyevsky as philosophical detective story, and he notes that it is also like a Socratic dialog and profound political parable. The main quarrel he has is with Rand's hard line on charity.

Most of the other assessments, even those that found something to admire, were not unalloyed endorsements. The summation of the *Newsweek* review is that Rand presents a "powerful argument." Still, the reviewer calls the book "gigantic, relentless, often fantastic," in its "eloquent flow of ideas." In the "Talk with the Author" afterword to the review, Rand is quoted as naming the small group of disciples of her ideas "The Children," whom she sees as intellectuals capable of changing the world. Helen Beal Woodward's estimation is that "Ayn Rand is a writer of dazzling virtuosity." Woodward notes Rand's ability to leave a "powerful, disturbing impression." However, she also finds the book "shot through with hatred," and Rand's "considerable gifts" undone by her "prolixity and her incontinence." Woodward is one of the reviewers who saw the female fantasy level of the novel, calling it a "non-stop daydream" for girls who would like to see themselves as running a railroad with one hand while reducing men to "panting adoration" with the other.

Critics, even those generally receptive to Rand's message, are prone to question the efficacy of her tone and verbal effusion. Richard McLaughlin, writing for the *American Mercury*, is a case in point. He welcomes a polemic against "bureaucratic mumbo-jumbo" and the encroachment of the welfare state, but he is staggered to find the answer to his desires in the form of a "leviathan" that "often shouts at the top of its lungs." For all his sympathy with Rand's positions and advocacy of reason, he is put off by her "long-windedness," and although calling her "no literary giant," he is among the first to compare *Atlas Shrugged* to *Uncle Tom's Cabin*.

Perhaps when her more private correspondence or diaries are published, we will know exactly how Rand reacted to the fusillade of negative reviews. What we have now are the observations of people who were closest to her at the time. The novel made her wealthy and world famous. It accomplished the goals she had set for herself as a fiction writer, the creation of an ideal man and the world one wanted to live in. Contrary to expectations, according to Barbara Branden, Rand was not upset by the bad reviews; she expected them. What did dishearten her, sending her into a long period of depression, was the lack of support by any of the public figures she had expected to appreciate her accomplishment, to share her philosophy.

The general readership was obviously undeterred by critical hostility and derision. As was the case for *The Fountainhead,* the sales figures for *Atlas Shrugged* put it into the best-seller category. It has been in print since its publication. And while hostility has continued from many quarters, the book has garnered small but steady reassessment over the years.

These reassessments sometimes come from surprising quarters. *Reason,* a libertarian magazine, devoted a special issue to Rand's work in 1973. This is significant because Rand was openly hostile to libertarians, calling them, among other things, "hippies of the right."[7] "The New Republic" is Douglas Den Uyl's essay in *Reason.* In it, he makes an analogy between Plato's *Republic* and Rand's *Atlas Shrugged,* finding a number of ways Rand's work fits in the tradition of Plato's, particularly in her emphasis on virtue. The following year, *Reason* came out with Robert Greenwood's charge that critics and reviewers had failed to come to terms with Rand's novel, seeing that in the reviews of *Atlas Shrugged,* "misrepresentation and vituperation" are substituted for any attempt to identify the ideas of the novel and debate them. My own late-seventies article "Ayn Rand and Feminism: An Unlikely Alliance" grew organically out of teaching women's studies courses. My students were becoming depressed by the parade of betrayed, frustrated, ineffectual heroines who populated the pages of American fiction. The seventies were a time of search for "role models," and my students could not find one, even in novels that were being touted as breakthroughs of feminist fiction. Dagny Taggart's success both in running her railroad and in attracting the most heroic of men and the antisacrificial message of the novel qualified it, in the opinion of my students, as an appropriate text for women's studies courses.[8]

Rand expressed hostility to what she called "Women's Lib" in several of her newsletter articles. Undaunted by her hostility, feminist critics have continued to find ways to appreciate her fiction. The 1999 publication *Feminist Interpretations of Ayn Rand* contains several articles that suggest productive ways to reread *Atlas Shrugged*. Karen Michalson reads Rand's novel as a "feminist creation myth," finding Dagny Taggart "arguably one of the strongest heroes in Western literature." Michalson's essay is subtitled "The Epic Hero/ine in Disguise." In the same volume, Judith Wilt's "The Romances of Ayn Rand" examines how Rand's novel represents "the furious exasperation of the precocious girl denied access to the world of doers and makers." The novel is, in Wilt's assessment, "strenuously meritocratic" and naive in its equation of virtue with success, but she values the "exalted love of one's own life" it exhibits. "Fluff and Granite: Rereading Ayn Rand's Camp Feminist Aesthetics" is Melissa Jane Hardie's singular contribution to a revisionist approach to Rand. Hardie's essay posits Rand as a camp persona, an ersatz movie queen, who borrowed heavily from melodrama. Hardie sees in a feminist rereading of Rand a strategy that corresponds to one of "camp's most important functions: to liberate unexpected meanings from unorthodox materials."

Writing shortly after Rand's death in the early eighties, Robert Hunt begins his reading with the opinion that "Ayn Rand is a prophet whose time has come, gone, and come again." His essay, a chapter in an anthology about works of science fiction and fantasy, assesses *Atlas Shrugged* as the "most powerful and influential work to emerge from the American Right." Hunt rejects Rand's contention that her purpose is not the philosophical enlightenment of her readers; he defines *Atlas Shrugged* as an "apologue, an argument for an intellectual and moral position, which happens to take the form of a novel." He also argues that the "novel's bulk ... is actually an asset to its function as an apologue."

The Other Fifties: Interrogating Midcentury American Icons, an anthology published in 1997, includes an essay by Stacey Olster entitled "Something Old, Something New, Something Borrowed, Something (Red, White, and) Blue: Ayn Rand's *Atlas Shrugged* and Objectivist Ideology." Olster locates Rand's "strike" strategy as one she shares with a number of novelists whose protagonists choose withdrawal rather than engagement, specifically, Ralph Ellison's invisible man, Joseph Heller's Yossarian, Saul Bellow's dangling man, and Norman Mailer's Barbary Shore. However, Olster finds Rand, unlike those leftist writers, more in tune with the eighteenth-century Founding Fathers and their belief in some form of "governing aristocracy as a stabilizing force in society."

In 1997 the Institute for Objectivist Studies and the Cato Institute cosponsored a 40th anniversary celebration of the publication of *Atlas Shrugged.* Little in the program addressed the literary qualities of the book. The program boasted businesspeople, philosophers, and a television commentator. All addressed the influence of the book in diverse areas such as business, economics, and politics.

One of the problems in qualifying the importance of Rand's magnum opus is that it does not fit comfortably into either of the two main categories used in academe to classify fiction. On the one hand, there is "serious fiction," those works of timeless quality that speak to the human heart about universal issues and that are the mainstay of literature classes. They are the canon, haute literature, art. They are taught in high schools and universities; their plots and characters are part of our common culture. Professors write critical articles about them in scholarly journals. On the other hand, there is popular fiction, generally written to appeal to the tastes of the time; its purpose is to entertain the reading public, thus ensuring the author's financial gain. The popularity of such works is often short-lived, although there is growing attention to them as part of popular culture studies. Serious literature lasts; best-sellers are usually evanescent. Paradoxically *Atlas Shrugged* is both. It was a best-seller in 1957 and has continued to sell well in all the years since that date. Still, it has transcended the best-seller category because of its durability, which makes it something of an anomaly. Even those who continue to question the novel's literary merit would have to agree that it is "significant," if not "serious," fiction. In that way, it is not unlike Harriet Beecher Stowe's *Uncle Tom's Cabin,* which, though it is not considered a book of great literary merit, is nevertheless a classic because of its political import. *Atlas Shrugged* is also a work that stirred a political movement in the United States. Stowe influenced abolitionists and fueled the antislavery movement; Rand is given credit for creating a philosophy and intellectual movement, Objectivism, and stimulating the nascent libertarian movement.

Counting Rand as an inspiration for the libertarian movement is not without its problems. She would have renounced the connections. Ayn Rand described libertarians as thugs and hoodlums, "whim-worshipping subjectivists." She rejected them and their political philosophy completely, and yet polls among libertarians reveal that she is "the most important intellectual influence on an entire generation of libertarians."[9] Many believe that Rand popularized libertarian ideas, bringing them to a wide audience because of the popularity of her fiction. Others have questioned the extent of Rand's influence in libertarian circles, claiming the influence is not so strong with the new generation as it was earlier. Still, *Liberty,* a libertarian and classical liberal magazine, regularly publishes articles dealing with Rand and reviews of works about her, as does *Reason.* And the Cato Institute, popularly referred to as a libertarian think tank, cosponsored the 40th anniversary celebration of the publication of *Atlas Shrugged.* It is important to point out that the celebration was a collaboration of Cato and the Institute for Objectivist Studies, which is an indication of the coming together of these two important areas of Rand's influence.[10] One of the sessions at this daylong celebration traced the influence of the novel on the market-liberal movement. The Ayn Rand Institute has continued to renounce all connections with libertarians.

The antipathy between Rand and libertarianism is curious. Joan Kennedy Taylor, who knew Ayn Rand personally, wrote that in the early days of Taylor's newsletter *Persuasion,* she had asked Rand how to credit the political ideas she was espousing. It was during the Goldwater presidential campaign of 1964. Taylor reports that Rand responded, "The name for my *political* philosophy is libertarianism."[11] Nathaniel Branden, on the other hand, remembers that Rand was suspicious of the term as early as the late 1950s. In his remembrance, Rand said that the political philosophy she espoused was laissez-faire capitalism. He recalls that for all his arguments in favor of the term "libertarianism," especially defined as one based on the inviolability of individual rights and the rejection of initiation of force, Rand still rejected it as sounding "too much like a made up word."

On a personal level, *Atlas Shrugged* was the demarcation work that ended her career as a novelist and launched Rand as a popular philosopher. Ronald Merrill sees the novel as the "destination of her intellectual journey" (59). What he finds in the novel is the solution to the great question of her life—how a rational person functions in an irrational society. The novel expounds her "radically new philosophy" at almost every level, from metaphysics to epistemology to ethics to politics to economics to aesthetics.

Another area in which Rand's works had a noticeable effect is revitalizing the American individualist movement. In a time when col-

tion. Others have questioned the extent of Rand's influence in libertarian circles, claiming the influence is not so strong with the new generation as it was earlier. Still, *Liberty,* a libertarian and classical liberal magazine, regularly publishes articles dealing with Rand and reviews of works about her, as does *Reason.* And the Cato Institute, popularly referred to as a libertarian think tank, cosponsored the 40th anniversary celebration of the publication of *Atlas Shrugged.* It is important to point out that the celebration was a collaboration of Cato and the Institute for Objectivist Studies, which is an indication of the coming together of these two important areas of Rand's influence.[10] One of the sessions at this daylong celebration traced the influence of the novel on the market-liberal movement. The Ayn Rand Institute has continued to renounce all connections with libertarians.

The antipathy between Rand and libertarianism is curious. Joan Kennedy Taylor, who knew Ayn Rand personally, wrote that in the early days of Taylor's newsletter *Persuasion,* she had asked Rand how to credit the political ideas she was espousing. It was during the Goldwater presidential campaign of 1964. Taylor reports that Rand responded, "The name for my *political* philosophy is libertarianism."[11] Nathaniel Branden, on the other hand, remembers that Rand was suspicious of the term as early as the late 1950s. In his remembrance, Rand said that the political philosophy she espoused was laissez-faire capitalism. He recalls that for all his arguments in favor of the term "libertarianism," especially defined as one based on the inviolability of individual rights and the rejection of initiation of force, Rand still rejected it as sounding "too much like a made up word."

On a personal level, *Atlas Shrugged* was the demarcation work that ended her career as a novelist and launched Rand as a popular philosopher. Ronald Merrill sees the novel as the "destination of her intellectual journey" (59). What he finds in the novel is the solution to the great question of her life—how a rational person functions in an irrational society. The novel expounds her "radically new philosophy" at almost every level, from metaphysics to epistemology to ethics to politics to economics to aesthetics.

Another area in which Rand's works had a noticeable effect is revitalizing the American individualist movement. In a time when collectivist ideas reigned in everything from pedagogical techniques to group therapy, Rand's staunch individualism gave succor to those who found themselves in the intellectual minority. This was particularly so in universities and colleges that became increasingly leftist. It is telling that Ayn Rand societies sprang up on college campuses, as did Objectivist clubs. Rand's influence can also be noted in free market foundations and organizations such as the Society for Individual Liberty and South Africa's Free Market Foundation. Bookstores that specialize in pro-freedom literature routinely feature not only works by Rand but books about her. Laissez Faire Books in San Francisco and Second Renaissance Books in Connecticut are two of the most prominent.

Rand's influence is noticeable in a variety of disciplines. Discussion of her ideas is not restricted to literary journals. In fact, if anything, Rand's importance has been acknowledged as often and more readily in philosophical and social science studies. The *British Journal of Political Science* cites Rand as one of the most important "rights" theorists. This categorization is also made in Norman Barry's book *On Classical Liberalism and Libertarianism.* On the other hand, John C. Merrill lists Rand with great thinkers who have influenced journalism. Few articles about Alan Greenspan, chairman of the Federal Reserve Board, fail to mention Rand's role in his early thought formation. She is listed in a book extolling the virtues of famous people with the courage to doubt. The number of master's theses and doctoral dissertations on her work has grown tenfold in the last 15 years.

In one of the final chapters of her biography of Rand, Barbara Branden names individuals who have affirmed the importance of *Atlas Shrugged* in their lives. It is a diverse group. Anne Wortham, author of *The Other Side of Racism,* credits the novel with her "psycho-intellectual transformation" (*PAR,* 408). Henry Mark Holzer, a constitutional lawyer and professor of law, found reading Rand like "taking a post-doctoral course in mental functioning" (409). Billie Jean King, who transformed women's tennis, told a *Playboy* interviewer that *Atlas Shrugged* was the novel that turned her around. It gave her the emotional ammunition she needed to win her battles both on and off the court.

There is strong evidence to suggest that Rand clearly meant the book to have influence beyond what one would expect of an ordinary novel, that she projected the possibility of its use as a foundation myth. As its creator, she understood her importance. Nathaniel Branden remembers her telling him, "All of the world's major religions have, in effect, their own mythology—tales, parables, stories of various kinds that are intended to dramatize and illustrate values and precepts. Although that is not how the novel started out in my mind, that is what it developed into—a mythology that concretizes, by means of the actions of its characters, the meaning of my philosophy" (*MYWAR*, 199).

READINGS

4

Plot

Complicated and intricate, a model of integration among story, characters, and theme, the plot of *Atlas Shrugged* has been described in a variety of ways. James T. Baker, for one, comments on the difficulty in classifying it, calling it, among other things, "both satire and deadly social commentary." One reviewer labels the novel a work of science fiction, another calls it a mystery story, and a third a female fantasy novel. For still others it is a profound political parable. As a work of social philosophy, it has been compared to George Orwell's *1984*. Donald Klopfer, the co-owner of Random House, categorized *Atlas Shrugged* as a moral defense of capitalism. Rand's novel is any and all of those things.

Fortunately, the reader does not have to choose among these different evaluations to enjoy the book. Rand's plot is complex and multilayered enough to allow it to work on many levels at once, and there is story enough to satisfy a variety of tastes. For those who read mostly for story, there are mystery, excitement, dead-end leads, and a profusion of plot twists and turns. For those who read at the deeper philosophical level, Rand provides, through her characters and in lengthy speeches, a working out of many of her basic philosophical principles.

John Steinbeck, commenting about his masterpiece *The Grapes of Wrath,* wrote: "There are five layers in this book; a reader will find as many as he can and he won't find more than he has in himself." A similar observation can be made about readers of *Atlas Shrugged.* Although there are some who may insist on a singular reading, most will find that Rand's multiple plotlines serve to enlarge the dimensions of the reading experience and that these multiple approaches to the plot enrich each other. Rand herself promoted the concept of a plot that can be read at multiple levels; she called them "tiers or layers of depth."[12] What follows are some possibilities for alternative readings of *Atlas Shrugged.*

AS MYSTERY STORY

"Who is John Galt?" is the question that begins *Atlas Shrugged.* Answering that question occupies a major part of the first half of the plot. Who is the inventor of the motor Dagny Taggart discovers in the ruins of the Twentieth Century Motor Company? Seeking the answer to that question occupies a key role in Dagny's quest to keep her railroad running through all the power shortages affecting the country. Why are there so few competent workers? Who is the "destroyer" who precedes Dagny in her search for the remaining productive and capable individuals, convincing them to quit just when she needs them the most? Although neither the reader nor the heroine is aware of it, the answer to all these questions is one and the same. One way of approaching the story is in terms of the puzzle plot, a subgenre of the traditional mystery or detective story. And therein lies much of the ingenuity of Ayn Rand's stratagem. The reader replicates Dagny's search, putting first one, then the next, piece of the puzzle in place, never quite getting the whole picture, till every piece has been found.

"Who is John Galt?" is the query that initiates the plot. It is a question that serves as a catchphrase to embody the unease and apprehension of the populace of the United States as it is depicted in the times of *Atlas Shrugged.* It is a rhetorical question, one that requires no response. It connotes the unanswerable. Characteristically, the phrase also provides summation to a litany of despair such as "Nobody can help what he does, that is the way things made him. There is nothing we can do about anything. ... What's the use anyway?" (*Atlas Shrugged,* 146). It also means "Don't ask questions nobody can answer" (23). In other words: Who is John Galt?

Like any good mystery writer, Rand provides well-hidden clues to the answer throughout the story. Answers are offered by various characters, some more and some less credible. An unnamed woman at a party given by Lillian Rearden claims that John Galt was a millionaire who while sailing his yacht on the Atlantic Ocean saw the sunken towers of Atlantis and chose with his crew to sink the ship and join the hero-spirits who lived there (147). Francisco d'Anconia chuckles and affirms that the fool woman "doesn't know that she was telling you the truth" (147). In the context of all the other seemingly more important party chatter, the reader may easily overlook this clue.

In another scene early in the novel, Dagny abandons her brother, jumps out of a car, and seeks shelter in a small diner. The diner is pictured in darkness, with windows that present "a bright band of glass and light" (167). The image is reminiscent of the Edward Hopper painting *Nighthawks*. A bum in the diner tells Dagny that he knows that John Galt was an explorer, the greatest that ever lived. He found the fountain of youth at the top of a mountain, and after ten years of agony trying to bring the fountain back to men, he found that it cannot be brought down (169).

Francisco d'Anconia does not represent John Galt as an explorer who was successful where Ponce de Leon failed, but instead he makes an analogy to Greek mythology. He tells Dagny, "John Galt is Prometheus who changed his mind" (480). D'Anconia explains that John Galt is a Prometheus who has withdrawn his fire—until men withdraw their vultures. The analogy is problematic. In d'Anconia's characterization, it is men, not Zeus, who set the vultures on Prometheus. The implication is that humanity has not appreciated the gift of fire and therefore Prometheus is withdrawing it. This is consistent with the themes of the novel because in the novel, it is the lesser beings, the unproductive and the second-handers, who are unappreciative of the talents and abilities of the "titans," the Prometheuses of society. It is they—men—who create the vulturous laws and restrictions to inhibit the productive, punishing them rather than rewarding them for their gifts. In the myth, however, it is not man, the beneficiary of Prometheus's largesse, but Zeus, from whom he stole the fire, who punishes Prometheus. Prometheus is punished not by lesser beings that are unappreciative but by a greater being for stealing something that belongs to the gods and allows humans to improve their miserable existences. It is for this defiance of inexorable omnipotence that Prometheus became such a hero for romantic writers. Individualistic and atheist poets such as Byron and Shelley wrote paeans to Prometheus, Byron hailing his "impenetrable Spirit" and his encouragement of the mind, Shelley projecting his ultimate triumph over Zeus.[13]

In another instance of the well-disguised clues Rand sprinkles throughout the story, Dagny speaks with Dr. Robert Stadler about the reliability of Rearden Metal. He offers, as an example of hope turned to disillusionment, the story of his three brilliant students. One, Francisco d'Anconia, has become a dissolute playboy; the second, Ragnar Danneskjöld, has become a pirate. The third, whose name Stadler unaccountably deletes, has "vanished without a trace—into the great unknown of mediocrity. He is probably a second assistant bookkeeper somewhere" (182). Stadler's statement resonates with dramatic irony, but this early in the plot, the reader is still trying to comprehend, as is Dagny, what is happening to the country, what accounts for the shortage of able workers; and so it is easy to miss the clue. Later, in another context, Stadler tells Dagny: "I knew a John Galt once—only he died long ago. He had such a mind that, had he lived, the whole world would have been talking of him by now." Dagny responds, "But the whole world is talking of him" (336). As bright as she is, it is a wonder that she does not connect the John Galt of this story with the other students Stadler has named—students whose names she does know. Why doesn't she ask Francisco who his other classmate was? Dr. Robert Stadler is also supposed to be brilliant. How does he not make the connection between his brilliant student and the engine model Dagny has shown him? An astute connoisseur of detective fiction would have asked this question, but most readers do not have enough clues this early in the novel to make the necessary connection. It is also to Rand's credit as a mystery writer; a true crafter of the genre drops clues and foreshadows events in such a subtle manner that when the denouement occurs, the reader responds, "Of course, I should have known that."

In a gesture of defiance that exemplifies Dagny's battle against the palpable futility, fear, and despair infecting the country, Dagny names the line she builds with Rearden Metal the John Galt Line. The line is a success, counter to all expectations. At a press conference, she answers a reporter's query of "Who is John Galt?" with the declaration "We are" (224). Francisco reacts oddly to the naming, and in an ominous bit of foreshadowing, he warns Dagny that John Galt may come to claim his railroad if she names it that. His prediction is prophetic. Eventually Galt does.

The success Dagny achieves in the battle to build the railroad culminates the first stage, or complication, in the plot. Once Dagny accomplishes this task, the next problem she takes on arises out of a curious discovery she makes during a trip with Hank. They take what is supposed to be a break from their hectic schedules and end up exploring an abandoned factory. In it, Dagny uncovers the ruins of an extraordinary motor. Struck by the enormous potential of the motor, she begins a search to discover its inventor. She vows, "I'll find him— if I have to drop every other thing I'm doing" (271). She believes that the inventor is the "most important man in the world" (307). Hank Rearden tells Dagny, in another of those clever uses of dramatic irony Rand employs so effectively, that the inventor must be dead. If he were alive "the whole world would know his name by now" (271), which of course it does.

Over and over, in the story of Dagny's search for the inventor, Rand uses dramatic irony to foreshadow the conclusion to the mystery. Looking at the motor and musing about its inventor, Dagny thinks that a mind like the one that created the motor would know how to win the battle she is waging to keep her railroad running and to keep the country afloat. The irony here is, of course, that ultimately John Galt does know how to win the battle, only it is not in the way Dagny anticipates. Hank Rearden tells a clerk in the Hall of Records, "We're looking for a friend of ours" (274). He, too, does not realize that he is telling the truth, that the man he finds will be one of his best friends. "I don't think you folks are detectives" (275) concludes Mayor Bascom of Rome, Wisconsin, to whom they go for information. But in fact, that is just what they are, detectives searching for clues to the identity not of a criminal but of an inventor.

The simultaneous searches to uncover the history of Twentieth Century Motors and the identity of the inventor of the motor lead Dagny to an interview with Ivy Starnes, one of the last owners. She, of course, does not remember the name of the first engineer to quit the company. In her code of values, being the embodiment of altruism and collectivism that she is, "He wasn't anybody important" (302). Dagny's search then leads her to Mrs. William Hastings, whose husband had been the chief engineer of Twentieth Century Motors. Dagny hopes she will find that he was the inventor of the motor. Although Mrs. Hastings knows of the motor, she explains to Dagny that "it was the invention of a young assistant of his" (304). This is Dagny's first positive clue to the identity of the inventor. Then Mrs. Hastings echoes the words of Dr. Stadler, remembering that her husband had predicted that the young man would "someday up-turn the world" (304). Although she does not remember his name, she does point Dagny in the direction of her next clue, an encounter with Hugh Akston and a cigarette marked with a dollar sign.

Dagny is not completely in the dark. She has glimmers of the answers to her questions. When she and Owen Kellogg find themselves on a frozen train, their conversation stirs her subconscious:

> Somewhere on the edge of her mind—like the wisps she saw floating on the edges of the prairie, neither quite rays nor fog nor cloud—she felt some shape which she could not grasp, half-suggested and demanding to be grasped. (626)

But she does not explore her intuitions. She is rushing to find Quentin Daniels, the only mind left in the country who might be able to replicate the achievement of the inventor of the motor. Of course, the destroyer has been there before her, removing Daniels before she can talk to him.

Ayn Rand, employing an adroit plot maneuver, has Dagny find the solution to her search, unexpectedly, at the moment when she thinks she has failed. Her detective work is about to pay off, but in a most surprising way. Grabbing a plane to give chase to the plane taking Daniels and the destroyer away, Dagny follows them. Flying over Colorado, she loses them, and her plane begins a dive she cannot control. As she crashes, her mind speaks the sentence she hated—words the narrator tells us that Dagny thinks of as "words of defeat, of despair and of a plea for help: Oh hell! Who is John Galt?" (643).

Those are the last words of part 2. *Atlas Shrugged* is now more than half over, and most of this plotline is resolved. When Dagny opens her eyes at the beginning of part 3, all her questions are answered. She looks into the face of John Galt. He is the inventor of the motor. He is also the one responsible for the disappearance of the productive and capable people. Not only that, but he does have a plan for reversing the despair and decline of the country. He is also the ideal man, the answer to her romantic search. The detective has literally fallen into the solution to her problem. The mysteries are solved.

In the essay "The Literary Method of Ayn Rand" (a chapter in *Who Is Ayn Rand?*), Nathaniel Branden wrote about another level of the mystery story. He quotes Rand calling it "a mystery story, 'not about the murder of a man's body, but about the murder—and rebirth—of man's spirit' " (98). Branden identifies it as a mystery to be solved by philosophical detection. Just as Rand dissolves the dichotomy between mind and body, between the spiritual and the material, so in this mystery story the line between the material and the philosophical mystery stories is nonexistent. The philosophical mystery story undergirds all.

Rand's tribute to Aristotle is evident in the titles of *Atlas Shrugged*'s three main parts, "Non-Contradiction," "Either-Or," and "A Is A." The philosophical mystery story operates at a different and simultaneous level with the material one. In *Structure and Meaning in Ayn Rand's Novels*, Kirsti Minsaas describes Dagny's quests to find the inventor of the motor and keep her railroad running as a "cover plot" to conceal the event of the major plot, which is the philosophical one.

David M. Brown also points out that all mysteries are not solved when Dagny lands in the valley and finds John Galt. Brown explains that one of the "deepest and most persistent mysteries of the novel," one that puzzles the reader as well as Dagny and Hank, is the mystery of why society has deteriorated as it has and "what kind of moral code could be the solution to the dysfunction." Brown notes that it is only in the full analysis provided by Galt's speech that the answer to that question is provided. According to Brown: "The ultimate mystery of the novel is the murder mystery about how man's spirit (or at any rate, the spirit of many individual men) was murdered." The speech also identifies the murder weapon: "the philosophy of altruism and rationalism."[14]

The philosophical mysteries that Dagny and Hank must solve involve understanding the seemingly contradictory nature of their experiences, choosing either to continue to work under impossible restrictions or to quit, and understanding that A is A.

As Science Fiction

The argument for reading *Atlas Shrugged* as a science fiction novel is based primarily on the fact that the setting seems to be a projection into the future. It is a future in which Rand posits what the country and the world would be like if they continued with certain practices and directions she discerned while writing the novel. Her main projections follow a political line, however, with minor nods to future technology. The novel was published in 1957, but the world Rand describes is not the world of 1957. There are certain recognizable geopolitical realities. The world and the United States are distinguishable, but there are notable differences. For one, the world is made up of "People's States." Among those named are the People's States of Argentina, Chile, England, Europe, France, Germany, Guatemala, India, Mexico, Norway, Portugal, and Turkey. The United States seems to be made up of the same geographically recognizable states and cities. A number of states, such as Arizona, California, Michigan, New York, and Utah, are named specifically, as are cities such as New York City and Washington, D.C., which is still the capital. Colorado is depicted in a positive light as the sanctuary for most of the productive people.

But whereas the geography of states and cities seems the same, the government is quite different. The country is led not by a president but by Mr. Thompson, the "Head of State." There is no House of Representatives and Senate; there is a "National Legislature." Given the general socialistic direction of governments in the 1950s, one can follow the reasoning behind Rand's projection.[15] In his "Chronology for *Atlas Shrugged*," Hans Gregory Schantz posits 1980 as the opening year of the novel, 1984 as the end.[16]

In terms of its technological milieu, however, there is a strange disjunction in this projected society. Rand has her productive characters create futuristic inventions, inventions that are still not extant some 40 years after the novel's composition. But in key respects the technology is decidedly backward looking, harking back to the early part of the century.

The seminal invention in the plot is Galt's motor, which, in Dr. Robert Stadler's words, solves the "secret of converting static energy into kinetic power." It powers Mulligan's Valley, creating electricity at a much-reduced rate. Although the motor is but half the size of a boxcar, it has the potential to replace the power plants of the country. However, the motor does not exist in the outside world, nor does any other kind of forward-looking energy source, no solar power, for instance. The reason Galt leaves the motor in ruins in the factory is that he invented it while he was working for Twentieth Century Motors. In the plot of the novel, no one in the outside world is capable of making it work there.

Another example of the advanced technology in the novel is Rearden's Metal, which Rearden has been working on for ten years. It has its first pouring in the context of the narrative. Rearden's invention is described as a metal alloy that is harder than steel, "a metal that would be to steel what steel had been to iron" (*Atlas Shrugged,* 35). Dagny Taggart orders it for use as railroad rails, but she also notes its potential for diesels, cars, planes, motors, and even chicken wire. The State Science Institute proclaims the new metal dangerous, but like many great innovators, Rearden is undaunted.

Ellis Wyatt, who restored his father's dying oil fields, is introduced early in the story. He has developed a method for reviving exhausted oil wells, something oilmen have still not been able to accomplish. In the valley, Wyatt has also developed a process for producing oil from shale, producing some 200 barrels a day while he devises methods for getting it even faster. Another futuristic invention is the ray shield that guards Mulligan's Valley from outside scrutiny. John Galt explains that it works by refractor rays, which project a reflection over the valley in much the same way a mirage is created on a desert. The image is refracted from a layer of heated air.

Although such inventions play crucial roles in the plot, there is not much else in the novel that projects a sense of what a future society might look like in terms of technology or industry. Most glaring in terms of its old-fashioned technological milieu is that Dagny Taggart, the protagonist, works in an industry more geared to the nineteenth than the twentieth century. The heroine works in the transportation industry, which is unaccountably dominated by railroads. Rand's failure of imagination in this choice is hard to justify. On the one hand, the major heroes develop new methodology and revolutionize their industries. On the other hand, Dagny's trains have stopped at the level of the diesel engine. Rand should have been aware that the future of transportation was in the air, not by train. Or, at least, the trains should have been jet-propelled. One can only speculate about the source of this imaginative limitation. The genesis may have been a personal limitation; we know that Rand never learned how to drive. Barbara Branden writes of Rand's fear of flying. She was able to control it long enough to take a flight to Portland, Oregon, to receive her honorary degree of doctor of humane letters from Lewis and Clark College (*PAR*, 318).[17] Airplanes are not absent from the novel. Rand does create several situations in which her heroic characters actually fly airplanes. One of the climactic scenes in the novel has Dagny, Francisco, Hank, and Ragnar rescuing Galt and returning him to the valley by airplane. However, the planes they fly are small propeller planes. Francisco's plane can be hid in the brush. But there is little sense of an airplane industry; there is no sense that people travel by plane. Rand's characters take trains. This is odd because the growth of the airplane industry was well under way by the time the novel was published. It was generally conceded that much of the future of transportation, not only for business and tourism but also for mail and packages, was in the air.

Another failure of imagination occurs in the scene where Dagny, finding herself on a stranded train, must walk miles to find a telephone. That a woman as enamored with high technology as Dagny would not have carried at least a walkie-talkie is inexplicable. Portable phones were not so hard to envision in that day and age if the writer was trying to envision the future. Even in the *Dick Tracy* comic strip, which every newspaper of her day carried, Tracy, an otherwise low-tech detective, had his combination watch–two-way radio. It was such a popular gadget that toys were made to replicate it.

Still another jarring note in this projection of a future world is in those instances, particularly those that are supposed to reflect key points in the plotline, where characters use anachronistic language. In most parts of the story, John Galt is well-spoken and courteous. In fact, when he first meets Dagny, although he has loved her from afar for more than a decade, he addresses her as Miss Taggart. On the other hand, when he is making a crucial comment about the direction of his strike, he says to Mr. Thompson, "The game is up, brother." Considering that Galt normally speaks in quite a different tone and level of usage, why would Rand make him sound like a thirties Hollywood gangster? "The game is up" reads like "the jig is up." Also, when Galt signals the end of his banquet speech, he says, "Get the hell out of my way." Perhaps this is meant to be forceful, profanity being a rarity in fiction of the time. Still, it is a pretty mundane and trite level of usage for the man who stopped the motor of the world.

Rand's use of the word "brother" as the term of address for the world of the looters is both effective in terms of her theme and problematic in terms of anachronistic language. "Brother, you asked for it!" (851) is the message Francisco puts on the sign on Times Square. "You asked for it" is what a movie gangster might say as he pulls the trigger in a shoot-out with a fellow gangster, or what a Hollywood detective would exclaim to indicate that the gangster's deeds result in his getting shot. In a more general context, referring to people as "brother" was a type of slang of the time. It corresponded with addressing someone as "guy" or "fellow." Later slang equivalents might be the usage of "man" in the sixties or "dude" in the nineties.

Kirsti Minsaas makes a cogent argument that Rand may be using the term "brother" ironically here to draw attention to her theme that man is not his brother's keeper. By addressing the looters of the world as "brother," Galt and d'Anconia point out that brotherhood is based on the trading principle, not on a sacrificial mortgage.

A counter to criticism of Rand's deficiency of imagination, in terms of the technology in her future world, is the idea that Rand is working not in science fiction set in a future world but in a subset of the genre that creates a plot set in an alternative reality, perhaps a parallel universe. If one reads *Atlas Shrugged* as an alternative-reality fable, then the mix of past and present with intermittent futuristic technology is not a lapse but in keeping with the conventions of the genre. This reading is strengthened by the fact that Rand is describing a world in collapse and degeneration. Every fourth store on Fifth Avenue is out of business. Even typewriters can't be repaired. Many of the innovators and inventors have dropped out. The strike of the men of the mind has been going on for more than a decade, so it could be expected that society would, of necessity, revert to older technologies. No date is ever specified, which adds to the sense of a parallel universe. Also, those in power, especially the government, promote stasis. The State Science Institute tries to keep Hank Rearden from producing his revolutionary metal; James Taggart is constantly thwarting Dagny's attempts to improve the efficiency of the railroad.[18]

Perhaps more than a science fiction novel, *Atlas Shrugged* can be characterized as a combination dystopian and utopian novel. The dystopian aspect dominates, and the utopian is present only during the brief time Dagny spends in Mulligan's Valley. The valley acts as a foreshadowing or model of what the world could be like. But that would be possible only if the society outside operated by the principles of the society in Mulligan's Valley, in particular its oath: "I swear by my life and my love of it that I will never live for the sake of another man, nor ask another man to live for mine" (675).

Rand's identification of Mulligan's Valley, or Galt's Gulch, with an ideal community is evident in her chapter names. The first chapter of this final section of the novel is "Atlantis." The second chapter is more specifically named, "The Utopia of Greed." But Galt's Gulch is only a blueprint of the utopia the strikers hope to build in the outside world because it has only a small number of people in it. Those who live permanently in the valley are there by invitation, and they are generally the most productive citizens who have dropped out of U.S. society. Many of the valley citizens spend only one month a year there, still living in the outside world most of the time. Their only restriction is that they must not let the outside world benefit from their great abilities, so they mostly do menial labor to sustain themselves.

The association with a utopia is also made at the dinner at Midas Mulligan's. Dagny sees the faces of the men of the mind who have disappeared from her world as set "against the golden sunburst of rays." The image is definitely celestial. She compares the encounter to a dream a child might have of heaven, where one might meet all the great people of history one would have wished to know (679). Professor Akston makes the specific connection to the possibility of creating a heaven on earth, not waiting for the afterlife.

The predominant dystopian aspect of the novel unfolds as the plot does. The reader is set in a vaguely familiar world. Things break down, and it is hard to get them fixed. People give excuses for their inadequacies. There is a superfluity of bureaus and committees. It seems all too familiar. Slowly, however, one begins to realize that it is not the present but some abstraction from the present. Rand's dystopia is a projection of what the world, and particularly the United States, will become if things continue on the path of choosing collectivism over individualism, altruism over egoism, and mysticism over morality. Like Orwell's *1984*, *Atlas Shrugged* is also a projection of the horrors of ubiquitous and intrusive government, but much of Rand's focus is on the economic realm and how that affects the personal. The ultimate dystopian touch is Directive 10-289, which ties workers to their jobs like slaves, forces businesses to stay open regardless of whether they are making a profit, and forces all patents and copyrights to be turned over to the government by means of "Gift Certificates." The directive also freezes the levels of production, consumption, wages, prices, and profits, symbolically freezing the world into a state of stasis.

Another quality Rand's dystopia shares with Orwell's is in the corruption of language. Orwell's totalitarian state creates "Newspeak" to manipulate the masses, declaring "War is Peace, Freedom is Slavery, Ignorance is Strength." Rand's parasites also use language to obfuscate and veil their true purposes, declaring the good of the people their primary goal when they really mean to serve only themselves. Language is a tool necessary for the development of concepts, and its betrayal is a key element in Rand's dystopia.[19]

Ultimately, however, Rand's attitude is optimistic. She projects a promising ending, a return to the principles on which the United States was founded. In this battle, the productive win.

As Female Fantasy and Feminist Fable

Nathaniel Branden, in his recollection of reading the manuscript of *Atlas Shrugged* while it was in progress, tells of teasing Ayn Rand about how few significant female characters there are in the novel. Her response, as he recalls it, was: "This is my fantasy. What do I need other women for?"[20] Rand was conscious of the element of fantasy in the writer's enterprise. In her journal notes about the creation of the novel, Rand verified her preference for the fantasy fulfillment achieved by being a fiction writer over what she calls the boredom of writing a philosophical nonfiction book. "In a book of fiction, the purpose is to create, for myself, the kind of world I want and to live in it while I am creating it."[21] If further corroboration is needed for a reading of *Atlas Shrugged* as a female fantasy novel, and in particular as the author's fantasy, Barbara Branden provides it. She remembers Rand describing Dagny as "myself, with any possible flaws eliminated."[22] It follows then, that if one reads the work as the fulfillment of Rand's intentions, *Atlas Shrugged* owes a good part of its appeal to the plot layer that reads like a female fantasy novel. In sum, Rand has concretized her philosophical principles in the characters and events of the story, primarily for her own enjoyment of living in that world she has created, and as a secondary consequence, she lets us enjoy it with her.

Judith Wilt describes the "stubborn bestsellerdom" of Rand's novels as evidence not only that Rand has projected her fantasy life in them but also that they reflect some "key components of the national fantasy life."[23] Wilt identifies the wish to live in it while creating it as the "foundation desire of romance." She makes the distinction that if one can no longer live in it after having created it, it is romance, whereas if one can live in it after having created it, it is philosophy. This is a balance she reads as a "sublime equipoise."[24] And this balance of romance and philosophy is key to Rand's fictive world.

As a male fantasy might create the situation of one man surrounded by numerous women, all desiring him, so Rand's female fantasy portrays the heroine projection of self as the object of desire for more than one man. In her previous novels, Rand had created romances in which two men love the heroine: Leo and Andrei in *We the Living;* Bjorn Faulkner and "Guts" Regan in *Night of January 16th;* Howard Roark and Gail Wynand in *The Fountainhead. Atlas Shrugged* enlarges the romantic triangle into a quadrangle. In this "sublime equipoise" of romance and philosophy, Rand has created a world in which the idealized projection of herself is surrounded by not just two but numerous heroic men, the best of whom are in love with her. The ones who are not in love with her admire and respect her ability. To add a touch of feminist icing to this utopian cake, the heroine is not only the object of desire of the men, but she is also a role model for self-defining, assertive, and competent womanhood.

Dagny Taggart is a heroine who is equal to any and superior to most of the male characters in the novel. Furthermore, as Karen Michalson asserts: "Dagny Taggart is arguably one of the strongest heroes in Western literature," one who operates on epic scale.[25] Susan McCloskey compares Dagny to Odysseus and Jesus as an epic protagonist engaged in a quest for reaching or finding home.

Rand's flight of female fantasy begins with a heroine who is a physical and intellectual paragon. Dagny Taggart is as capable as she is beautiful, and her quest for professional and personal fulfillment propels the plot. Dagny is introduced to the reader through the deliberately sexual semiotics of focusing first on her "leg, sculptured by the tight sheen of the stocking ... arched instep...feminine elegance" (*Atlas Shrugged,* 20). Before we know anything else about Dagny, we know that she has great-looking legs. A stocking-encased leg in high-heeled shoes is shorthand for sex appeal. This synecdochic substitute is a timeworn cinematic technique, whereby the camera signals feminine allure by showing the audience legs first, and then body, and sometimes only the legs. Filmmakers have used it since the early days of film. Lewis Milestone's screenplay for John Steinbeck's *Of Mice and Men* introduces the seductress of the story by focusing first on her legs, encased in black silk stockings and high heels. This technique was replicated with great success in the late-fifties television series *Richard Diamond, Private Detective.* The audience sees only the shapely legs and hears the voice of "Sam," Diamond's obviously attractive secretary.[26] In drawing attention first to Dagny's legs, Rand's narrative eye replicates what Laura Mulvey identified as the "male gaze" of the Hollywood camera.[27] This is not surprising, as Ayn Rand began her writing career in the United States creating scenarios for the movies.[28] Even when describing Dagny as a young girl, the narrator draws attention to her "long show-girl legs" (*Atlas Shrugged,* 100).

Dagny's mother is one of the first to recognize her daughter's physical beauty. Although Dagny has never shown interest in the things Mrs. Taggart considers important for a girl's socialization, inexplicably Dagny does decide to go along with her mother's plan for a formal debut. Surveying her chiffon-gowned daughter as she prepares for her first ball, Mrs. Taggart remarks, "Dagny, do you see how beautiful you can be when you want to?" (100). Mrs. Taggart recognizes that even at age 17, Dagny projects a woman's "confident, dangerous power" (101).

But Dagny is more than beautiful, and her looks are not of great moment for her. In a period when most girls were encouraged to devote an inordinate amount of time to the externals of appearance, Dagny acts as a feminist icon. She resists sex role socialization and refuses to be inhibited by looks or gender. In a nod to the existence of such restrictions, Rand allows her heroine the thought: "She was fifteen before it occurred to her for the first time that women did not run railroads and that people might object. To hell with that, she thought—and never worried about it again" (54–55). The sexist limitations she faces are illustrated by the fact that though she is obviously the best qualified to run Taggart Transcontinental, her father leaves the controlling interest to her brother James Taggart, who becomes the company's president. Dagny becomes the Vice-President in Charge of Operation. There is little impediment to Dagny's professional rise to that level because, in the world of the novel, men of talent are rare, and "she took positions of responsibility because there was no one else to take them" (55). In some ways, Dagny is like the female secretary or administrative assistant who keeps the company running while the male president gets the credit and big salary. Throughout the novel, Rand underlines the fact that Dagny should be heading the railroad, but the reader is not led to blame the problem on sexism. Inadequate men are in positions of power in all sectors of the society. Still, in comparison to the other women in the novel, Dagny represents a curiously avant-garde attitude for the time period. This was, after all, before the early works of the second wave of this century's women's liberation movement. *The Feminine Mystique* was not published until 1963, six years after *Atlas Shrugged*.

Three love affairs provide the romantic plot, and Dagny is a principal in all three. Her first love, which begins in childhood, is her relationship with Francisco d'Anconia. The story is told in flashback. Their families had been friends, and during their childhood, Francisco had spent one month of every year at the Taggart estate. There, he, Dagny, and Eddie Willers, who also spent his time there, form a youthful triumvirate. The three, always led by Francisco, experience a series of adventures, all meaningful in terms of the children's growth and development of competence. Francisco nicknames Dagny "Slug," and she and Eddie call him "Frisco." It is from Francisco that Dagny first hears the credo of competence she comes to share: "Dagny, there's nothing of any importance in life—except how well you do your work. Nothing. ... It's the only measure of human value" (98). But no matter how hard Dagny and Eddie try to learn some skill at which they can beat Francisco, they are never successful. He beats them at everything; he is always the winner. As the narrator explains, "Francisco could do anything he undertook, he could do it better than anyone else, and he did it without effort" (92). During their teens, childhood camaraderie grows for Dagny and Francisco into a full-fledged love affair, each being the other's first sexual partner. Francisco explains, "We had to learn it from each other" (103).

Rand's refusal to characterize the sexual relationship as shameful or sinful was part of her iconoclastic appeal in the still puritanical decade of the fifties, an era when writers put most female characters into the category of either Madonna or whore. Women who enjoyed sex outside the legal boundaries of marriage were considered tarnished. As Wendy Martin explains in her key analysis of literary heroines in American literature, "As daughters of Eve, American heroines [who] have dared to disregard authority or tradition in the search for wisdom or happiness ... are fallen women, eternally cursed for eating the apple of experience."[29] This bifurcation of fictional women into what Leslie Fiedler calls "Fair Virgin and Dark Lady" was seen by many critics as a manifestation of a need by the authors to punish women who defy the strictures of a patriarchal society and reward those who remain subservient to the system. Sexually autonomous women, where they exist in fiction, are punished by failure to thrive. In *Atlas Shrugged*, Hank Rearden, in his initial misguided state, articulates this concept, which he has absorbed from his society. As the narrator explains his thinking, he had accepted the doctrine "that women were pure and that a pure woman was one incapable of physical pleasure" (*Atlas Shrugged*, 153). Good women are chaste; bad women are sensual. Good women who choose to explore their sensual sides are punished. The punishment can take the form of dying in childbirth, à la Hemingway's Catherine Barkley in *A Farewell to Arms*, or committing suicide like Chopin's Edna Pontellier in *The Awakening*.

Rand's heroines defy these categories. Dagny Taggart, in particular, celebrates her sexuality, and her creator rewards her for doing so. Although American society in the fifties would have considered Dagny a fallen woman because she has sex outside of marriage, she feels neither demeaned nor stained by her relationship with Francisco. She revels in being his mistress. She knows instinctively that her desire for Francisco and his desire for her grow out of a mutual admiration and respect. "She knew, even though she was too young to know the reason, that indiscriminate desire and unselective indulgence were possible only to those who regarded sex and themselves as evil" (106). Rand's heroes and heroines are meticulously discriminating. If anything, some critics have questioned the realism of their long periods of chastity.[30] Rand's heroes and heroine are both physically appealing and mentally adroit, personifications of the unity of mind and body, and so their sexual desire is a by-product of their values and is thus a tribute to the one they desire.

As both Francisco and Dagny go about building their careers, they see each other only intermittently. At one point, she does not see him for three years, but she is not unhappy because she understands that they are both on a road to becoming leaders in their chosen fields and that sometime in the future they will be together. The rupture comes when she is 24 years old.

Francisco invites her to dinner and to spend the night with him at the Wayne-Falkland Hotel. His behavior is inexplicable to her; he says things, warns her not to be astonished by anything he does, all of which becomes understandable as the plot unfolds. Before she leaves, he tells her not to wait for him, that the next time they meet, "you will not want to see me" (112). Subsequently she reads about him in the newspapers, stories of his sybarite existence, lavish parties, and numerous affairs. But Dagny survives the disappointment. She equates leaving Taggart Transcontinental with suicide, but the same is not true about being left by the man she loves. She gets over it.

According to Lord Byron, "Man's love is of man's life a thing apart, / 'Tis woman's whole existence." Among the variety of reasons that *Atlas Shrugged* is an appealing mix of feminist and romantic fantasy is that Dagny, the heroine, does not exemplify this attitude. In an era when most women had been convinced to concentrate their lives on men who in turn concentrated on work, an ethos Edith de Rham calls "The Love Fraud," Dagny never considers giving up her life's work for any man.[31] Even John Galt, who has persuaded the greatest business and industry leaders in the country to abandon their work, cannot convince Dagny to give up her railroad. Having fallen in love with him and seen the utopian valley where he and the other heroes live, she still chooses to return to the world and try to salvage Taggart Transcontinental. In Ayn Rand's hierarchy of values, a woman's work is as important to her as a man's is to him, and this does not preclude a satisfactory love life. Therein lies some of the feminist appeal of this novel, for Dagny Taggart leads the life of a feminist role model.[32] As much as she loves Francisco, her self-esteem is such that she has no doubt about her ability to survive without him. Hurt as she is by the loss of this first love, Dagny has never made life with Francisco her primary goal. "She found the clean, brilliant sense of life as she wanted it—in her work" (*Atlas Shrugged,* 113). She is whole unto herself; she does not need a man either to complete her or to give her identity. Late in the novel, of course, we learn that Francisco has staged all the affairs and that he has remained true to Dagny, in both mind and body.

A good part of the novel, and for many readers the most complex and interesting of the love stories, is devoted to the development of Dagny's relationship with Hank Rearden. Their love story generates interest both because of the obstacles the lovers must overcome professionally and personally and because of Hank's misguided attitude toward sex. In this novel, ironically, it is Hank Rearden who initially espouses the attitude that there is a divorce between the pleasures of the spirit and the pleasures of the body. He has internalized the attitude that sees sex as sinful. Hank views his desire for Dagny as degrading. He tells her, "I wanted you as one wants a whore—for the same reason and purpose" (238). Dagny, who understands the single genesis of his respect and desire for her, tells him that she is happy to be the instrument of his pleasure. Later, as Hank begins to understand more, they encounter the sleazy Mayor Bascom, who tells them, "In this world either you're virtuous or you enjoy yourself" (277). He is expressing Hank's former mind-set, and that of the predominant society.

In Rand's hierarchy of values, romantic love and its physical expression are inextricably connected with one's values. People who have self-esteem choose partners who represent the achievement of their values. People with low self-esteem choose partners who allow them to feel superior or to fake it. There is no mind-body dichotomy for people of integrity. The love stories in *Atlas Shrugged* are all illustrations of this theory.

In one scene, Francisco d'Anconia, acting as Rand's spokesman on this subject, tells Hank Rearden, who has equated his sexual desires with degradation, that there is no conflict between the standards of the mind and the desires of the body (455). Francisco explains that "a man's sexual choice is a result and the sum of his fundamental convictions. Tell me what a man finds sexually attractive and I will tell you his entire philosophy of life" (455). Dagny explains it in a different manner. She explains to Hank that when a man wants her, he rises in her estimation. "I feel that others live up to me, if they want me" (351). This is contrary to the reaction of most people, who rise in their own eyes if others want them.

This conception of the blindest passion of the body coming from the clearest perception of the mind allows Dagny to continue loving Francisco and Hank after she meets her ideal mate, John Galt. Because with each of her lovers, the passion grows out of a shared sense of values that do not change, they can continue to love and desire each other, even though they will not act on their desire. This allows for one of the most appealing aspects of this fantasy for women. Dagny, as she moves from one love to the next, never loses the love of any of the men in her life. When Hank realizes that she has fallen in love with someone else, he tells her, "What you'll give him is not taken away from me" (793). Hank also tells her, after he meets John Galt, that he does not blame her for her choice. Dagny tells Hank that she will always love him and that she feels she has committed no treason to either of them.

Adding to the decidedly romantic and fantasy-fulfilling aspects of the novel is the fact that John Galt, who has struggled valiantly for 12 years to achieve his goal, is willing, in the final days of the struggle, to risk his life to gain Dagny (747). Against the wishes and the counsel of his friends, he returns to a rapidly deteriorating situation on the outside. Dagny herself tells him it will be too dangerous for him to be there, though she is the one who inadvertently leads the villains to him. And even then he tells her that he would have been disappointed if she had been able to keep away from him. Of course, Rand does not feel bound to have one or both of her great lovers die, which is generally the case in the archetypal tragic story of star-crossed lovers such as Romeo and Juliet or Anthony and Cleopatra. Another feminist twist to this romantic roundelay is that Dagny is part of the rescue team to save Galt from his torturers. Unlike the preponderance of romantic heroines of her or earlier times, Dagny does not spend her time crying and screaming about the situation. She wields a gun and shoots it. This has raised some eyebrows, as she is the only one in the group to kill someone, and that someone is more confused than villainous.

Rand creates numerous fantasy-fulfilling situations for her heroine. She not only puts Dagny into progressively more satisfying love affairs with three out of the four major male characters in the novel but also makes her the only woman in a male Round Table of competence and productivity. When Dagny lands in Mulligan's Valley, everyone there welcomes her. At a dinner party at Midas Mulligan's home, she is the only woman in a group of seven men, each representing a high level of accomplishment. They are Richard Halley, the composer whose music provides the triumphant theme song of the novel; Judge Narragansett, representing the top jurist; Ellis Wyatt, an innovative oilman; Ken Danagger, from the mining industry; Hugh Akston, exemplifying the best in the professorial ranks; Dr. Hendricks, from the world of medical science; and Quentin Daniels, a young physicist. Dagny is presented as "Taggart Transcontinental," and they all acknowledge her greatness, telling her, "Well done" (679).

The fantasy is not uniformly satisfying, nor is the feminism unalloyed.[33] There are troublesome areas for readers, feminist and nonfeminist alike. Many of the lovemaking scenes can be read as privileging the rougher aspects of sexual satisfaction. Imagery of conquest and contempt abound. Francisco, though he obviously loves Dagny, often looks at her with a "mocking glance." First he kisses her, then he smiles "down at her confidently, derisively" (109). Dagny awakens from her first sexual encounter with Hank "with a bruise above her elbow, with dark beads that had been blood" (237). The act itself is described as being "like an act of hatred" (235). Of course, Hank's contemptuous smiles and mocking looks, as well as his violence, can be rationalized because in the early days of the relationship, he is disgusted with himself for his desire and tells her that she is as vile an animal as he is. Dagny not only submits to being thrown down on her knees and having her arms twisted behind her back till pain rips through her shoulders, she relishes it. The narrator tells us that Hank knows "by the eagerness of her movement as her arms seized him, that this is the way she wanted to be taken" (252). When he learns that Dagny and Francisco have been lovers, Hank seizes her with such violence that "she felt prepared to accept that he would now kill or beat her into unconsciousness" (593).

Dagny and John Galt resist consummating their relationship in the cleanliness and comfort of his home in the valley. Instead he follows her down a dark, abandoned train tunnel in the bowels of the city, and they couple on broken sandbags, covered with burlap. Her teeth sink into the flesh of his arm; his elbow knocks her head aside and his mouth seizes her lips "with a pressure more viciously painful than hers" (880).

In "Looking through a Paradigm Darkly," Wendy McElroy probes the meaning of these rough and violent love scenes, scenes that have been likened to rape. McElroy explains that before and after these scenes there is clear indication that Dagny has given tacit if not explicit consent. McElroy reminds us that the sexual couplings of Rand's heroes and heroines are not like the passive surrender portrayed in most romance novels. The paradigm is much more one of equality, more like the irresistible force meeting the immovable object, with the immovable object choosing to make a slight adjustment. In Rand's sexual model, "enraptured surrender" is the epitome of female satisfaction.

It should be noted that regardless of the number of times Dagny "surrenders" sexually in this novel, her yielding does not affect her professional goals or her personal decisions. She does not hang around, wait for his call, or even suggest marriage. She goes on with her life. The poetic imagery suggested by mating in Rand's fantasy is more in keeping with Andrew Marvell's "To His Coy Mistress":

> Now let us sport us while we may,
> And now, like amorous bird of prey,

. . . .
Let us roll all our strength and all
Our sweetness up into one ball,
And tear our pleasures with rough strife
Through the iron gates of life:
Thus, though we cannot make our sun
Stand still, yet we will make him run.

Even when Dagny is presented the opportunity of living happily ever after, as it were, with her ultimate love object, John Galt, in the Edenic valley, she chooses to leave him and continue her fight for her railroad.

Read from the female perspective, *Atlas Shrugged* presents both positive paradigms and fantasy fulfillment. Its heroine begins as an intelligent, capable, and independent woman. After adventures and love affairs, she is, if anything, wiser, capable enough to take on the challenge of rebuilding the railroads, and still very much her own woman.

AS ARTHURIAN ROMANCE

Rand identified herself as a romantic writer, and it is not unfitting that in the development of her literary tastes, French writers predominate. This is appropriate because the romance as a literary genre is of French origin. Rand's preference for French romances developed in her childhood. Young Alisa found her first fictional hero in a French children's magazine serialization of Maurice Champagne's *The Mysterious Valley*. This hero, about whom she spoke often, was Cyrus, the strong, purposeful, and defiant British officer. He is a character who became the prototype for her ideal heroes. In her teen years, Victor Hugo became an abiding favorite. Rand recalls, in particular, the character of Enjolras, who though not the central protagonist of *Lès Misérables,* was the figure who answered her literary needs for an inspirational character. The works of Hugo, particularly in the heroic sense of life they projected, were an important influence on her direction as a writer. Nathaniel Branden remembers her saying, "Even his villains are heroic" (*MYWAR*, 78). In her mature years, Rand wrote an introduction to Hugo's novel *Ninety-Three*. The French playwright Edmond Rostand's *Cyrano de Bergerac* was her favorite play. Rand's literary French connection is incontrovertible.

If one can name these specific French authors and works that influenced Rand's literary tastes, there are other unnamed influences that reach further back into the Western romantic tradition, influences that may have helped concretize her mental images of the heroic. One finds in the French romantic concept of the heroic some tenuous support for the fact that in *Atlas Shrugged* there are strong resonances, if not a provable direct influence, of one of the earliest traditions of French romance, one reaching back to the eleventh century.[34] Rand does not make any specific allusions to the Arthurian romance cycle or to the courtly love ethic in the plot, characters, and themes of *Atlas Shrugged*; however, there are definite parallels.[35]

In classical mythology, Atlas is the titan who holds up the world; in Arthurian legend, Arthur is the king who, in some future time, will return to save it. But whereas Atlas is a lonely figure, Arthur is not. Much of the appeal of the myth of Camelot is that Arthur does not act alone; he gathers a company of heroes to help him in his quest. And although Rand uses analogies to both Atlas and Prometheus in her novel, given the number of heroes of lesser and greater stature that Galt assembles for his quest, an analogy to Arthur might be equally suitable. In the Arthurian cycle, other knights often play as large a role as Arthur does. In some accounts, Arthur is even relegated to background figure. In *Atlas Shrugged* the stories of Rearden, d'Anconia, and Danneskjöld are foregrounded. The details of Galt's quest must be inferred or recounted secondhand.

Like King Arthur, John Galt creates an assemblage of heroic men around him to accomplish their shared goal. The myth of Camelot continues to speak to us and has inspired numerous past generations because of its image of the pursuit of a dream of a better and brighter world. Arthur rose out of a dark age to epitomize the determination of the human spirit to overcome great odds, to pursue a noble path, regardless of the cost. Galt's strikers arise in a new dark age, imbued with equal fervor for the right.

Nowhere is the Round Table image as telling as in a scene in Mulligan's Valley, Rand's alternate Camelot. Dagny Taggart is invited to the house of Midas Mulligan. The name is apt because, like Arthur, Midas was a mythological king. The valley is, in a sense, his kingdom, since he owns it. At this dinner, the assembled "knights" eat off of silver trays. Their chairs are placed on Oriental rugs; there is Renaissance art on the wall; and though there is no table, they sit about the room in a manner conducive to their sharing the details of their quests with Dagny. As Dr. Hendricks, Judge Narragansett, Richard Halley, and Hugh Akston recount for her the story of their journeys from the outside world to the sanctuary of Mulligan's Valley, they are not unlike the individual knights of Arthur's Round Table, whose singular feats are recounted at the assemblies of the whole.

In Rand's novel, John Galt is an Arthur figure who is "the once and future king," simultaneously the answer to the world's problems and the fulfillment of Dagny's dreams. He is also a Galahad figure, the pure knight who will achieve the Grail. Coincidentally, the first three letters of Galt's and Galahad's names are the same. In the Arthurian cycle, many great knights quest for the Grail, but none of them is pure enough of heart to attain it. In terms of the story line of Rand's novel, John Galt's dedication to his quest is so focused that he has had no time for a romantic life. Like Galahad, he is a solitary, virginal figure until late in the plot when the fulfillment of the quest is ensured.

If John Galt is at once an Arthur and a Galahad figure, Hank Rearden fills the role of Lancelot. This is in keeping with Rand's French literary antecedents, because the most influential work in the French Arthurian tradition is Chrétien de Troyes's *Lancelot*. Lancelot, like Rearden, is not initially one of Arthur's knights. He must prove himself and win a place at the Round Table. And it is in this story of Lancelot that the courtly love concept is added to previous Arthurian tales. What distinguishes Chrétien's *Lancelot* from the Arthurian tales that preceded it is that this poem foregrounds the adulterous relationship between Lancelot, King Arthur's premier knight, and Queen Guinevere. Likewise, a primary plotline in *Atlas Shrugged* highlights the adulterous relationship between Dagny Taggart and Hank Rearden.

The adulterous relationship is a mainstay of the courtly love tradition that developed in a time when marriages were economic and political arrangements. In the tradition, love is an ennobling passion and inspires heroic impulses in the lover so that he can prove himself to his lady. For Rand, too, love is an expression of one's highest values. The intensity of the love affair is heightened by its necessarily secretive nature. Like the courtly lovers, Hank and Dagny must keep their relationship secret. The twist here is that it is Hank who requires the secrecy because he is the married one. Like the knight and courtly lover, Hank showers his lady with precious gifts.

In the Arthurian cycle of stories, the relationship between Lancelot and Guinevere has destructive consequences for Camelot. To defend her honor, Lancelot must challenge his chivalric brothers. Sometimes knights are pitted against knights, brother against brother. In Malory's version of Arthur's saga, this adultery brings down Arthur's kingdom. The adultery in *Atlas Shrugged* also has destructive results, though not as definitive. Because Hank fears the consequences to Dagny's reputation, he is blackmailed into signing over his great invention, Rearden Metal. Thus, symbolically, his kingdom of steel mills is brought down by his adultery.

In the Arthurian saga, to protect their adulterous relationship, Lancelot must meet all challenges to Guinevere's virtue. In doing this, he kills or gravely wounds many a virtuous knight, some who had been his close friends. Such is the case, symbolically if not figuratively, in *Atlas Shrugged*. And though the adulterous relationship in Rand's novel does not pit knight against knight in physical combat, it does create a situation where the main knights of the story inflict wounds on each other. Hank Rearden is hurt by his discovery that Francisco had been Dagny's lover. Instead of challenging Francisco to use a lance in a tourney, Rearden slaps Francisco's face. Then Rearden performs a symbolic joust, with a phallic lance, in a sexual union with Dagny that Rand's narrator describes as an "act of victory over his rival ... his conquest of that man by means of her body" (*Atlas Shrugged*, 593). Even the normally imperturbable John Galt is jolted to find out that Hank Rearden and Dagny Taggart are lovers. The reader learns of this only by Eddie Willer's comment to Galt after revealing the news. In previous scenes, the face that Eddie talks to is described as serene, but after Galt receives this news, Eddie has to ask, "What's the matter with you?" (603). Eddie Willers, though he is more squire than knight, is also dealt a blow, described as inflicting pain "to the point of physical torture" by his discovery of the affair (600).

There are other connections between courtly love and Arthurian legend that apply to a reading of *Atlas Shrugged*. As it developed in France, courtly love was a complex product of many factors, among which are the social, religious, philosophical, and erotic. Its literary appearance constituted a revolution in thought and feeling, particularly in relation to the position of women. It is not coincidence that this literary convention flourished in the courts of Marie de France and her mother, Eleanor of Aquitaine. In *Atlas Shrugged*, Rand presents a philosophy of love and sex that is an integration of many factors and, like its Arthurian predecessor, has had an influence on the position of women. As in the courtly love ethic, Rand idealizes passion and promotes the sovereignty of love. Francisco swears an oath by the only woman he ever loved. But Rand modernizes the heroic themes of love and nobility to include women. Her message of productivity and satisfaction through a job well done is for both sexes. Unlike the heroines or ladies of early romances, Rand's protagonist does not wait for her knight in shining armor to ride to her rescue; instead she rescues him, becoming, in effect, one of the knights.

T. S. Eliot's *The Wasteland*, which is linked to the Grail myth, is set in a sterile world replete with fear, disgust, and barren lusts. A similar atmosphere permeates the world of *Atlas Shrugged*. In the archetypal fertility myth of the Grail quest, drought and desolation are brought to the land, and neither man nor beast is fertile or productive. The land can be restored only if a "questing knight" goes to the Siege Perilous and asks certain ritual questions. The ritual question in

Plot

Rand's contemporary wasteland is "Who is John Galt?" Its answer restores productivity to a desolate land. Eliot paints a picture of a modern wasteland in overwhelmingly pessimistic tones, ending unaccountably with a benediction. Rand's more optimistic picture of a wasteland on the road to restoration has within its frame a prescription for a brighter future.

5

Characters:
A Study in Black and White,
Few Shades of Gray

The characters in *Atlas Shrugged* fall into easily identifiable categories. As a writer, Ayn Rand provides little if any interpretive room for readers to do their own evaluations. In this she is unlike the predominant naturalistic and realistic writers of her time; she does not withhold narrative judgment. Ambiguities and unfolding development are rare. What we see the characters do and their subsequent dialogues only serve to reinforce the narrator's preliminary presentation. Rand's narrator directs our judgment in all cases. This method of characterization has stimulated considerable criticism. Helen Beal Woodward complains of Rand's "stylized vice-and-virtue characters," calling them little more than dummies on which to drape ideas. Bruce Cook's objection is that the Randian hero is "idealized and exalted to the point where he simply does not exist on a recognizably human level." "Characters conceived in the crudest emblematic terms" is Robert Hunt's evaluation of Rand's characterization methodology. Whether it is spelled out in the first description or through a hint provided by name choice, there is no doubt about whether a character is virtuous or evil. Much like the allegorical characters in morality plays, Rand's characters are personifications in name and often physique of the qualities they embody. Richard McLaughlin calls them allegorical figures that serve as spokespeople for both sides of major social and moral arguments. Ayn Rand explained that her characters are "persons in whom certain human attributes are focused more sharply and consistently than in average human beings."[36]

A PANTHEON OF HEROES

Ayn Rand declared that an author's choice of subject is a representation of what that person regards as important. As an example, she used one of her favorite authors, Victor Hugo, who presented the triumph of heroes in his novels. She does the same in *Atlas Shrugged*. In keeping with her version of romanticism, Rand peoples her story with characters who are not just protagonists, people one might know or meet, but larger-than-life heroic projections of her ideals. In this she saw herself as creating a vision, not of things as they are, as would a writer of realism, but of things as they ought to be, in accord with her definition of romanticism. Nathaniel Branden explained her method of characterization as working not with a camera, like a photographer, but with a chisel, like a sculptor. This is in keeping with Rand's artistic premises of fiction, as opposed to history or biography. She is not interested in the question of whether her heroic characters exist in real life. Her characters are meant to represent potential, beacons of what humans might be.

Dagny Taggart is the main protagonist-heroine of the novel. Although there are other important and heroic characters, the narrative line of the novel details and follows Dagny's story more than any other. The reader's attention is focused on Dagny as she struggles to understand the forces that undermine her battle to run Taggart Transcontinental and build the Rio Norte Line; the plotline follows her through three romantic relationships and to eventual triumph.

Dagny is the embodiment of Rand's conception of the ideal woman in a way that none of her other female characters is. In discussion, Rand explained that her original plan was to create Dagny as a feminine equivalent of Howard Roark, the heroic protagonist of *The Fountainhead*. Dagny can be seen as a feminine equivalent of Roark, but as a fictional character, she is developed in much deeper detail and rounded where Roark's character is sometimes flat. The reader encounters Roark, Athena-like, full grown and mature. There is little sense of his development or motivation. Dagny's character unfolds in multidimensional complexity. First she is presented as a child, planning her career direction, then in adolescence as she deals with her developing sexuality and the mores that govern young womanhood, and finally in full-blown womanhood. Although she represents an ideal, there is some realism in her characterization. She learns, she develops, she deals with disappointment and frustration.

What Rand accomplishes in the creation of this unique character is considerable. Dagny Taggart has no equivalent in contemporary fiction. As an idealized figure, she is probably the most admirable and successful heroine in American fiction, serving as a fictional role model in many ways. Karen Michalson argues that Dagny is an epic "hero/ine" in disguise, the first in American literature. The problem most readers have had in recognizing Dagny as such is that "there's really no difference between her and her male counterparts" (Michalson, 217). The strong and active qualities she exhibits are traditionally thought to be masculine, both by other characters in the novel and by some readers, among them some feminists. The amalgam of what are traditionally thought to be masculine and feminine qualities in this one character inspired Thomas Gramstad to see Dagny as a character who presents the opportunity to go "beyond androgyny," to expose the flaws of traditional gender views.[37] Barbara Branden calls Dagny "the woman thought to be impossible in the conventional view of life—the woman engineer, dealing with the material world of metal rails and freight cars and diesel engines, who is, simultaneously, consummately feminine" (1999, 28). Readers have found much to admire in Dagny Taggart.

Rand's ideal of womanhood is a person of extraordinary accomplishment. She plays a central role in the economy of the country, running the transportation system that is its lifeblood. There is no doubt about her worth. Not only do Dagny's allies acclaim her value, but even her enemies acknowledge her exceptional abilities. Although her title is Vice-President in Charge of Operation, she runs Taggart Transcontinental. Her brother James Taggart is the titular head, but everyone knows that she is the one who makes things run.

Dagny's ideal qualities are not restricted to professional talents. She is not only capable; she is also attractive. Dagny is in her early thirties when the narrative begins, young looking, slender, with shapely legs, and medium-length brown hair. The narration underlines the fact that she does not look the part of a railroad tycoon. Her authority derives from her ability, not her title or her heritage. She is the granddaughter of the founder of the railroad, and she has a strong sense of her heritage.

The narrative finds her living a solitary personal existence. Her first lover was Francisco d'Anconia. They had been childhood friends, but his inexplicable transition into a playboy leaves her hurt and dismayed. Love comes into her life again when she accepts the challenge of rebuilding the Rio Norte Line (which she renames the John Galt Line). In the process, she develops both a business and a romantic relationship with Hank Rearden, a steel tycoon, who helps fund the line. Although he is married, she becomes his mistress. Together they try to keep the national economy from falling apart. Dagny fights longer than do any of the people of accomplishment against giving the world over to the "moochers and looters." Even after she meets and falls in love with John Galt and understands the nature of his strike, she will not give up her railroad. Rand explains Dagny's error as "over-optimism and over-confidence" (*J*, 424). At the conclusion of the novel, Dagny and Galt, along with the other people of the mind, are ready to return and rebuild the world.

If Dagny is the focus of the narrative, John Galt is the prime mover. She struggles with a situation he has created. He has vowed to stop the motor of the world and is slowly removing all the capable people from contributing their abilities to powering the economy. To run her railroad, Dagny must find qualified workers at all levels of the industry. John Galt keeps removing them from in front of her.

Galt belongs in a category of his own. He is more icon than character. To borrow a term from Hemingway criticism, Galt is the ideal hero, or "code hero," of *Atlas Shrugged*. Rand called him the culmination of her purpose of creating an ideal man. As such, he is the embodiment and exemplar of Rand's most cherished values. However, *Atlas Shrugged* presents his story only obliquely. The narration does not reveal his development and maturation, nor are we in his perceptions as he struggles to understand the cause and purpose of his struggle. We learn only secondhand about his enlistment of friends and other like-minded individuals.

Although he is not the chief protagonist, John Galt is the prime mover in terms of both plot and theme. It is he who stops the motor of the world when he leads the men of the mind on strike against all the leeches and parasites they have been sustaining throughout history. It is Galt who as a young engineer at Twentieth Century Motors revolts against the collectivist credo and says, "I will put an end to this, once and for all" (619). Although the reader encounters that story only after other plotlines have been initiated, its significance is clearer as events unfold.

Galt is a prototype of American aristocracy. He is self-made and self-educated. Unlike his two best friends, Francisco d'Anconia and Ragnar Danneskjöld, Galt is not the scion of a noble bloodline. In fact, he is curiously unconnected by familial ties, a Prometheus unbound. In his youth, John Galt leaves his home somewhere in Ohio and becomes the most promising young physicist ever to matriculate at Patrick Henry University. Faced with the implications of the situation at Twentieth Century Motors, he calls his friends, Francisco and Ragnar, to join him and become flame-spotters. Their task is to search out flares of genius, the capable and productive of society, and convince them to join the strike.

In keeping with his heroic stature, his physical appearance is hard and gaunt, his body suntanned. He has chestnut brown hair and deep, dark green eyes. Most telling of his virtuous status is a guilt-free face, the sight of which inspires instant recognition and respect from Dagny. That face also identifies him as the unknown worker for Taggart Transcontinental who wins Eddie Willers's trust. With Willers as an unwitting accomplice, Galt is able to undermine Dagny's efforts to keep capable people working.

Galt does not appear, except in disguise, until a little more than halfway through the novel. However, he is Rand's spokesman, and in his challenge to the villains to relinquish their hold on the government, he delivers a 60-page speech that is the philosophical crux of the story.

Ironically, Dagny has thought of Galt as "the destroyer" when in actuality he is the builder of the motor that will power the world and a prime force in the building of Mulligan's Valley, an ideal community in the mountains of Colorado. Rand saw Galt as "the proper integration of a complete human being ... a combination of an abstract philosopher and a practical inventor; the thinker and the man of action, together" (*J,* 480).

If Dagny Taggart is Rand's creation of an ideal woman and John Galt her ideal man, Hank Rearden is her symbol or abstraction for the martyred industrialist. Rand had originally envisioned Hank Rearden as an older man, and the character of Philip was to be his son, not his brother. But as the plotline developed, Rand decided that a romance between Dagny and Hank would facilitate her presentation of the connections between sex and economics. Their romance became a central plotline, a line that tied the whole plot together.

In the shorthand of Rand's character development, hard and lean are good, soft and flabby are bad. Thus Hank Rearden, like John Galt, is described as gaunt. Prominent cheekbones and the sharp lines of his face reflect a hard strength, accentuated by a lack of expression. He shows little overt emotion. His eyes are ice blue, his hair ash-blond.

But accomplished as he is, Hank Rearden is a man of little self-understanding. He is an industrialist of tremendous ability, an inventor who perfects Rearden Metal, an alloy stronger and more flexible than steel, and yet he is an unhappy man who does not know why he is unhappy. Judith Wilt describes him as a kind of female icon in the novel, living in a kind of schizophrenic shuttling between an unendurable family life and a profoundly satisfying work life. "He makes the classic 'female' adjustment: he accepts the world's definition of his work life, love and productivity as guilt and his withdrawal of pure love from his family as shame" (1978, 61). A perfectionist, he looks for fault in himself, unable to understand the attitudes of those who claim they love him.

For all his ability, Hank is the one who must learn the most in the novel, and his education occupies a goodly part of the plot. First, Dagny must teach him about the unity of passion and values. He marries Lillian because he thinks she is someone to attain. Full of self-doubt, having internalized the predominant definition of lust as sinful, when Lillian proves frigid, Hank convinces himself that his desires are depraved. He does not understand the nature of his passion for Dagny, initially, because he is one who is convinced of the mind-body dichotomy. As the relationship develops, he showers Dagny with lavish gifts: a pear-shaped ruby, a blue fox cape, gold bracelets, and fine crystal. But still he feels guilty, and it is this guilt about his love for Dagny that permits Lillian to manipulate him and cripples his ability to judge others.

In the course of the novel, both Dagny and Francisco give Hank the insights he needs to rise to a greater self-awareness, and he begins to rebel against his self-imposed martyrdom. His climactic moment is the delivery of a speech during a trial where he is accused of breaking one of the government directives that did not allow him to sell his metal to whomever he wanted. In his refusal to recognize the court's right to dispose of his property without his consent, he delivers a consummate defense of capitalism. Although his feelings for Francisco d'Anconia are strained by Francisco's superficial public image, their friendship grows until Hank learns that Francisco could have prevented a disaster for Rearden Metal but chose not to intervene. Once Hank learns about Mulligan's Valley and becomes one of the strikers, he is among people who appreciate his value and who will be friends worthy of him.

To make her message global, Rand wanted other nationalities and geographic locations to be represented in her story. If John Galt and Dagny Taggart are from the Northern Hemisphere, then Francisco d'Anconia represents the Southern Hemisphere. He is an Argentinean of Spanish descent. Born to aristocracy and wealth, Francisco d'Anconia begins in his youth to develop his considerable natural abilities. He takes a variety of odd jobs. The family tradition is that every d'Anconia, since the first ancestor fled the Inquisition, must earn the right to the name and leave the family fortune larger than when he received it. Francisco sets out to accomplish that goal. Rand presents him as a man with great joie de vivre. Tall, slender, dark haired, and blue-eyed, he carries himself with style; he looks the part of nobility. To emphasize his romantic demeanor, the narrator describes d'Anconia as looking as if a cape were unfurling behind him. While still in college, he works his way from furnace boy to factory owner, and by the age of 23, he is the copper king of the world. Then inexplicably, he changes. At age 36, he has the reputation of a dissipated playboy. He seeks out Hank Rearden and, despite Rearden's reservations, becomes his friend. Unbeknownst to Rearden and the reader, Francisco has assumed the role of reeducating Rearden, both to defend him and to convince him to become one of the strikers. To that end, d'Anconia delivers several of the most important theoretical speeches in the novel: the oration that contains the title imagery and the renunciation of the money-is-the-root-of-all-evil concept. He tries to convince both Hank and Dagny to stop placing their abilities at the service of second-raters. However, Rand structures her plot in such a way that d'Anconia is interrupted before he can do so. Francisco pays the highest price for his ideals: he loses Dagny first to Rearden and then to John Galt, and he destroys his family business, the d'Anconia mines. Nevertheless his strength of character and devotion to his ideals make him capable of absorbing all the losses and still reaping joy from his existence.

If Galt and d'Anconia represent the Northern and Southern Hemispheres, then Ragnar Danneskjöld represents the Old World as opposed to the New World, the Eastern as opposed to the Western Hemisphere. He is one of the triumvirate that sets out to stop the motor of the world. Ragnar is of European aristocracy. He first meets his lifelong friends, Francisco d'Anconia and John Galt, when they are all freshmen at Patrick Henry University. Rand describes Ragnar as an incredibly beautiful man with hair of gold and the audacity of a buccaneer. The paradox of his personality is that though he is a gentle and delicate intellectual, whose chosen field is philosophy, he becomes a pirate, sinking ships laden with foreign aid or important raw materials. There is a price on his head, and he is rumored to hide in an old Viking hideout in a Norwegian fjord, but none of the world navies seem able to catch him. Sometimes he operates on land, as when he blows up Orren Boyle's furnaces to prevent Boyle from using the ill-gotten formula for Rearden Metal. Ragnar turns the contemporary understanding of the Robin Hood myth on its head. Rather than steal from the rich and give to the poor, he steals from those he considers to be undeserving and gives to the deserving, creating accounts to return "loot" to the productive from whom it has been taken. Danneskjöld's part in the novel is minor compared to d'Anconia's, Rearden's, or Galt's, but as an ideal, Ragnar completes the picture of how men of ability and integrity must respond to a world of moochers and looters. He is married to one of the few beautiful and competent women in the novel, the actress Kay Ludlow, and their marriage is an illustration of a relationship of equals.

In *Atlas Shrugged* most of the able and virtuous people join the strike of the mind and become deserters. If they have not joined the strike before the time line of the novel, they join it in the course of the narrative as "the destroyer" convinces them of the validity of his approach. Dagny Taggart and Hank Rearden are the last holdouts.

Owen Kellogg is the first dropout Dagny encounters in the course of the plot. He comes to tell her that he is quitting because he had promised her he would notify her if he did. Of course, she does not know, and he does not tell her, the real reason he is quitting, that he has become one of the strikers. He is a young engineer who was an assistant to the manager of Taggart Terminal in New York. Dagny offers him a promotion, offers to let him name his price, but much as he loves his work, he refuses. To her question of why, he answers, "Who is John Galt?" Later she meets Kellogg on a frozen train, unaware that he is trying to make his way to Mulligan's Valley, where she sees him again. Like some of the other strikers, Kellogg lives on the outside most of the year, doing menial jobs, in order not to allow the moochers and the leeches to use his brainpower.

In the course of the plot, as Dagny and Hank struggle to keep the economy running, Rand interweaves stories of men such as Dan Conway, Ken Danagger, Ellis Wyatt, and Quentin Daniels. They are examples of productive people in a variety of fields who for one reason or another quit or become strikers. Dan Conway, who for a while is Taggart's chief competitor in Colorado, is a square and solid man near 50 who runs an efficient line, the Phoenix/Durango railroad. The "anti-dog-eat-dog" rule runs him out of business, so he retires to his ranch in Arizona. Danagger represents the coal industry. Rand portrays him as the prototypical American self-made man. He started as a miner and rose to become the owner of Danagger Coal in Pennsylvania. He is in his fifties at the time of the collectivist takeover. Opposed to the crippling government restrictions, he conspires with Rearden to provide needed coal and is thereby indicted, along with Rearden, for subverting government orders. Although he loves his work and his mines, Danagger retires and leaves the mines to no one. Without his brainpower, the mines become nonproductive, an object lesson in the need for the prime movers. The natural resources are still there, but it takes the person of ability and ingenuity to use them.

Ellis Wyatt is in the business of reviving old oil wells and making them produce again. He is young, quick-tempered, and able. A loner, he invites Dagny and Hank to dinner and to spend the night at his home at the conclusion of the first run of the John Galt line. When the crippling directives are issued, he destroys Wyatt Oil, setting fire to the oil fields, and vanishes into Mulligan's Valley. Wyatt's Torch, which is what the people name the one oil well that keeps on burning, is a key symbol in the novel, representative of his inextinguishable Promethean fire, one mere humans cannot put out.

Quentin Daniels is brought to Dagny's attention during her search to find the inventor of the motor. Daniels is a young physicist who has refused to work for Dr. Stadler at the State Science Institute but agrees to try to help Dagny reconstruct the motor. He resigns his job with her because he doesn't want the motor to be used in the service of tyranny. It is when she is trying to keep him from disappearing that Dagny crashes into the valley.

Some of the productive and capable people move full-time into Mulligan's Valley, the novel's utopia. Some spend only their vacations in the valley. They are careful when working on the outside to take only such jobs as will contribute only minimally to making things work. Mostly it is by doing manual labor, so as not to contribute their brainpower to the economy.

A key inhabitant of the valley is Michael "Midas" Mulligan. Mulligan had been the richest man in the country, a banker. He owns the valley where all the able and competent have gathered to build their own Atlantis and await the downfall of the collectivist state. He sells plots of land there to various of the strikers. The valley bears his name, and he runs a bank there where all exchange is done in gold. He quits the banking world when money is doled out on the basis of need rather than ability.

Hugh Akston, surrogate father for John Galt (and to a lesser extent Francisco d'Anconia and Ragnar Danneskjöld), had been their philosophy professor at Patrick Henry University. Akston is one of the last advocates of reason in the halls of academe, a believer that contradictions do not exist. He quits academia "in protest against intellectuals who teach that there is no intellect" (*J,* 631) and works in a diner when he is not in the valley. It is at his home that Dagny is presented with the rationale for the strike.

Rand demonstrates in this utopian valley that the capable are also adaptable. Whereas Calvin Atwood had been the owner of Atwood Light and Power Company of New York City, in the valley he becomes the owner of Atwood Leather Goods Company. Lawrence Hammond is the last producer of good cars and trucks in the outer world. Hammond, the owner of Hammond Car Company in Colorado, retires to run the grocery store in Mulligan's Valley. Roger Marsh owned a factory of electrical appliances near the town of Marshville. He tries not to desert but eventually does. He grows cabbage in Mulligan's Valley. Judge Narragansett, once the judge of the Superior Court of Illinois, runs a chicken and dairy farm in Mulligan's Valley. He quit the bench when a court of appeals reversed his ruling that those who earn are more entitled than those whose only claim is need. He would not uphold injustice. Ted Nielsen is the owner of Nielsen Motors, who quits and disappears when the John Galt line is closed. In Mulligan's Valley, he works as a lumberjack. Dwight Sanders is a maker of good airplanes and owner of Sanders Aircraft. In the valley, he becomes a hog farmer and plane attendant. Andrew Stockton is one of the people whose profession does not change in the valley. He has the Stockton Foundry there as he had it in Stockton, Colorado. Stockton is an eager competitor who is anxious to hire the sort of people who might one day be his most able competition.

A dinner party at Mulligan's house is the occasion for Dagny to meet Richard Halley, the composer whose heroic music is the theme song for the novel. Halley is a composer of intrepid, rebellious, and inspirational music. In the outside world, he had achieved acclaim after many years of struggle, but he retires the day after the success of his opera *Phaethon*. Also there is Dr. Thomas Hendricks, a great surgeon, who retires and vanishes after medicine is put under state control. Dr. Hendricks treats Dagny after her crash landing in Mulligan's Valley.

The only woman in the valley who is named and described in any detail is Kay Ludlow. She is an unusual beauty who had been a movie star. She is married to Ragnar Danneskjöld and waits in the valley while Ragnar risks his life. In the valley, she performs plays by authors unknown to the outside world. Dagny meets a few other women as she explores the valley, but they are not named. One is the woman who owns the bakery shop. She has chosen motherhood as an avocation and thereby produces joyous, healthy, and active children. Another is Rand herself, making an appearance as a fishwife and writer whose works would not be published because she "believes that when one deals with words, one deals with the mind" (*Atlas Shrugged*, 720). Barbara Branden calls this cameo a "Hitchcock-like appearance" (*PAR*, 229).

The outside world is not totally devoid of virtuous and capable people who have not joined the strike. Rand provides us with thumbnail sketches of them. Rarely do they appear more than once in the plot. Such is Mr. Ward, the fourth generation of his family to run Ward Harvester Company in Minnesota. It is a small, solid company, and Mr. Ward is ready to sell at a loss if it means keeping his doors open. He comes to Hank Rearden because he cannot get steel, and Rearden gets it for him. Bill Brent is the chief dispatcher for the Colorado Division of Taggart Transcontinental who warns Mitchum about the possible tunnel disaster, refuses to sign the order to send the

Comet through the tunnel, and quits rather than be forced to do what he knows is wrong. Tom Colby is the rolling-mill foreman and head of the Rearden Steel Workers Union, a company union. But he quits when Directive 10-289 is declared. Mrs. William Hasting is the dignified widow of the man who was chief engineer of the laboratory at Twentieth Century Motors. She is a serene woman who gives Dagny the clue that leads her to Hugh Akston. Pat Logan is the engineer of the Taggart Comet on the Nebraska Division who wins the lottery to drive the first run of the John Galt line on rails of Rearden Metal. The fireman on the same run is Ray McKim, described as large, grinning, and confident. Dick McNamara is among the best contractors in the country. He is one of the first of Dagny's business associates to walk out, quitting with a pile of contracts and a three-year waiting list of clients.

Two creations stand out among the briefly sketched positive characters. Gwen Ives is Hank Rearden's calm and efficient secretary. She breaks down in tears when she hears of the passing of the Equalization of Opportunity Bill. As originally conceived, she was to be an exact parallel of Hank Rearden except on a lesser scale. At a crucial juncture in the plot, Dagny encounters Jeff Allen. He had been a skilled lathe operator who cannot find an honest job and therefore becomes a hobo. Dagny meets him at the moment when the train conductor has just ordered Allen to jump off the train. Instead, she invites him to be her guest, and he is the one who tells her the story of Twentieth Century Motor Company. When the train is frozen, Dagny leaves him in charge.

Three of the most appealing characters in the novel represent how statist regimes destroy what is good in the human spirit. In discussing these people, who are basically good but have been either mislead or misinformed, Ron Merrill makes the point that in crisis situations, the ablest can often escape and make new lives for themselves. He likens Tony ("Wet Nurse"), Cherryl Brooks Taggart, and Eddie Willers to the people who perished at Auschwitz and Vorkuta because they either lacked the ability to fight the system, gave in to the experience of a horror beyond despair, or could not bring themselves to start over. Such people are, he thinks, the object of Rand's pity. Certainly, her portrayal of them is touching. Unlike the majority of minor characters who are presented in thumbnail sketches, presenting a flat, if positive, appearance, these characters are allowed a little development. They change in the course of the story.

When Cherryl meets James Taggart, who she thinks is the unsung hero of Taggart Transcontinental, Cherryl is 19, starry-eyed, and working in a dime store. She has dreams of bettering herself; she wants to learn. Initially she is so enthralled with Jim's attention that she drowns her doubts about him. She adopts his hostility to Dagny, until she learns, slowly and painfully, that Dagny is what she thought Jim was. Cherryl apologizes to Dagny, and Dagny offers her support, but Cherryl does not have the strength to cope with the horrors she encounters and thus runs through the darkness over a parapet to her death.

Wet Nurse (Tony) is initially put into Rearden Mills by Washington bureaucrats to act as an enforcer of government policies. The name "Wet Nurse" is given him by the steelworkers. He starts as a cynic who does not believe in absolutes. Rearden teasingly calls him Non-Absolute. But in response to what Wet Nurse observes, he comes to admire Hank Rearden, telling him to do as he pleases and that he will juggle the books so that Washington won't know. Wet Nurse eventually gives his life to protect Rearden's mills in one of the most touching scenes in the novel. According to Rand, Wet Nurse is a character who wrote himself, a rarity in her writing.

Eddie Willers is the average man. He plays a significant role in Dagny's life, as he is her chief assistant, one person she relies on. It is Eddie Willers who opens the novel, disturbed by a bum's question, "Who is John Galt?" Willers plays a crucial role throughout; his indiscreet revelations propel the plot. This he does by revealing to John Galt the information Galt needs to undermine Dagny's efforts. Willers's title is Special Assistant to the Vice-President of Operation of Taggart Transcontinental. Like his father before him, he is a retainer of the Taggart family. Willers wants to do whatever is right, to reach for the best that is in him. Fair, direct, and fiercely loyal to Dagny and Taggart Transcontinental, he cannot bring himself to quit. We do not know his fate. The story leaves him on a stranded train.

SQUADRONS OF SCOUNDRELS

Villainous characters swarm over the blighted landscape of *Atlas Shrugged* like maggots on a dead host. This is in keeping with Rand's theme of a world sucked dry by parasites as the productive are shackled or driven underground. As Rand intended, the novel is about the world, not just a few individuals. Given this global perspective, it would not be sufficient to have but one overarching villain. More are needed, and Rand provides a multitude of monsters. Parasitism in *Atlas Shrugged* is pandemic and necessitates scoundrels in many walks of life, miscreants of lesser and greater malevolence. The scope of Rand's unremitting invective is reminiscent of Pope's *Dunciad* or Dryden's "MacFlecknoe," which teem with satiric objects. Like Pope's Dunces, Rand's moochers and looters "rave, recite, and madden round the land." Rand's villains pullulate from every chapter, creating images not unlike the citizens of Hogarth's *Gin Lane* and the villagers in the works of Brueghel and Bosch.

In the creation of these human horrors, Rand adopts a traditional technique of comedy, which is the creation of humorous characters, that is, characters that embody one particular humor or personality trait. These characters' names are usually suggestive of that trait or characteristic. In comedy, some examples of this convention are the heroic Captain Absolute of Sheridan's *The Critic,* the nimble-fingered pickpocket Filch in Gay's *The Beggar's Opera,* and the lecherous Lady Wishfort and the treacherous Fainall in Congreve's *Way of the World.* Rand adopts the convention by naming a particularly parasitic character in *Atlas Shrugged* "Mouch" and another, who is obviously indicative of societal infection in need of lancing, "Boyle." Another way she uses names to indicate personality or predominant humor is by giving characters nicknames that suggest lesser stature or unpleasant noise. "Buzz," "Chick," and "Cuffy" represent these types. In the character of Tinky Holloway, Rand uses a nickname that is indicative of his diminutive stature and a last name that trumpets his hollow mind.

Not all characters fall into this convention of naming. Nor are all immediately identifiable by their physical appearance, though the reader is not left in suspense for more than a few sentences. Such is the case of the neutrally named Lillian Rearden. She is described as having an "exquisite profile," "lustrous" hair, and an "imperial beauty" (*Atlas Shrugged,* 39), but the narrator quickly qualifies the seemingly positive description. When the exquisite profile turns full face, the viewer is confronted with "vaguely pale" and "lifelessly empty" eyes, our windows to Lillian's soul.

Even in the case of the most minor characters, such as the unnamed, complaining passengers on the frozen train, physical shape mirrors and telegraphs the state of their inner beings. A woman who shrieks "with the demanding petulance of hysteria" (623) is described as dressed in a slovenly manner, coat thrown over a nightgown, slipping open to display a "protruding" stomach. Her manner is described as "loose obscenity" (624). A man who speaks to the heroine with a "tone intended for servants by a man unfit to employ them" is described as "bulky," with "too expensive an overcoat and too flabby a face" (624). Predominant descriptors of the villainous characters convey a sense of looseness, protruding and bulging physiognomy, pudgy and bloated appearance, what one critic has called an "apocalypse of goo." Everything about these characters is revealing of their negative status, from the way they look to the way they talk.

Human horrors abound in a plot that pits the productive against the parasitic. The parasites are divided into two categories: the looters and the moochers. Loosely defined, the moochers depend on the pity of the productive to supply their needs; the looters take what they want at the point of a gun, literal or figurative. One of the primary moochers is aptly named Wesley Mouch. He rises, appropriately, to the level of Economic Director of the country as it moves into a state of nonproductivity. Not so eminent moochers have such names as Chick, Buzzy, Tinky, Kip, and Bud. These diminutive nicknames bespeak their unsubstantial traits.

Dr. Floyd Ferris, who uses government threat and blackmail to take what he wants, personifies the looters. Ferris is ferretlike, a weasel who steals the work of others. He subtly threatens Hank Rearden that he and Ken Danagger could spend 10 years in jail because Rearden refuses to sell the State Science Institute 5,000 tons of Rearden Metal but has illegally provided Danagger with the metal.

Responding to the threat, Rearden observes, "In my youth, this was called blackmail" (405).

Five villains dominate the plot; three of them are closely connected to the major heroes, making the villains' perfidy that much more reprehensible. James Taggart is Dagny Taggart's brother. Lillian Rearden is Hank Rearden's wife. Dr. Robert Stadler is culpable because he was John Galt's, Ragnar Danneskjöld's, and Francisco d'Anconia's professor at Patrick Henry University. The other two archvillains are Dr. Floyd Ferris and Wesley Mouch.

We are introduced first to James Taggart, Dagny's brother and president of Taggart Transcontinental. He looks nearly 50 though he is only 39. Wan, petulant, and, irritable, his greatest fear is that he will be held responsible for anything. His posture is limp, his stance loutish, his eyes pale and veiled, his hair thin. He is a parasite of the first order, always relying on Dagny to get him out of trouble, attempting to ride Francisco's coattails to riches. If Rand's code holds that life is the primary value, then James is an example of one who values the opposite. He is a death worshiper, something he does not have to face till the end of the novel when the sum of his behavior is clarified for him by his encounter with John Galt. Throughout Taggart's life, he has rationalized to himself that his love for others and social duty have been his motivation, but he comes to see that "it was the lust to destroy whatever was living, for the sake of whatever was not" (1052). He leaves carnage in his wake. His marriage to Cherryl Brooks quashes her dreams, leading to her suicide. His is a need to cancel her "joyous eagerness to live" (1053). He marries Cherryl because he thinks she is beneath him and will therefore adore him, helping him fake a sense of his own worth. He and Lillian Rearden connive to keep Rearden in line. In Taggart's desire to kill John Galt, he finally comes face-to-face with his hatred of existence, a realization that leaves him "staring blindly," speaking in a voice that is no longer "the voice of a living consciousness" (1053).

Lillian Rearden is cleverer than James is, and in many ways more malevolent. His is a whiny portraiture, and his betrayals and machinations are more in the service of trying to maintain himself in positions of power or to help maintain his illusions about himself. Lillian, however, maintains no illusions. Her destructiveness is calculating. She determines to undermine Hank's sense of self-worth, to keep him in check. She belittles him, inviting Bertram Scudder, who has attacked Hank in print, to their anniversary party. Sarcasm, spite, and insults are delivered with a smile. She uses his virtues to provoke his guilt, putting upon him the responsibility for her happiness, though she will not say what would make her happy. She uses his sense of honor against him. Her sense of power comes from controlling and reducing that which is great. As she says, "If you had the most powerful horse in the world, you would keep it bridled down to the gait required to carry you in comfort even if it meant sacrificing full capacity" (372). She understands that a Hank Rearden operating without guilt at his full capacity as a human being would not be controllable.

If the mind is celebrated in this novel, then it stands to reason that the guiltiest villain is the most brilliant one, the one who knows the values and still chooses to betray them. Dr. Robert Stadler had taught that "the only sacred value in the world ... is the human mind, the inviolate human mind" (1027). He was the greatest physicist of his time, but he chose to sacrifice his integrity in order not to be bothered with material concerns. He allows his name to be used by the State Science Institute for bogus science. His mind and discoveries make possible the destructive potentials of Project X, but he does not denounce it. Stadler was modeled, in part, on J. Robert Oppenheimer, known as the father of the atom bomb, whom Rand had interviewed in the late 1940s, for a projected screenplay. She found him a fascinating, brilliant, and bitter man and even copied his office for her character Stadler.

Dr. Floyd Ferris has no previous relationship with any of the main characters. He comes into the plot through his manipulation of the system, representing government use and abuse of science. Rather than promoting scientific experiment, he uses the resources of the Science Institute to deride reason and logic in his book *Why Do You Think You Think?* Like Nazi doctors who performed horrific experiments on human subjects in the name of the advancement of medical science, Ferris's creative urges express themselves in the invention of the Ferris Persuader, an instrument of torture, fine-tuned to keep the subject in pain without killing him or her. He uses Dr. Robert Stadler, at first with feigned respect, but then with contempt, when Ferris knows Stadler is thoroughly compromised. Although Rand allows Ferris good looks, they are the antithesis to looks she admires. He is darkly handsome; his six-foot frame and mustache make him a Valentino type. Though he was the heartthrob of millions of women, Valentino is not listed among Rand's favorite Hollywood actors. Ferris uses science and technology for destructive, not constructive purposes, honchoing the deadly Project X, which demolishes everything within a 100-mile radius. But evil is eventually impotent in Rand's value system, and in the torture scene finale, Ferris is like an ineffectual grand inquisitor, breaking not his victim but his ally.

Wesley Mouch, who begins as Rearden's man in Washington, quickly betrays Rearden to become the Assistant Coordinator for the Bureau of Economic Planning and National Resources. James Taggart engineers the double cross. Squarish and pale, with a petulant lower lip and egglike eyes, Mouch never smiles. He rises quickly in Washington, advanced by mediocrity-loving people. When his programs don't work, he whines for greater powers. He pushes Directive 10-289 to achieve stasis and becomes the economic director of the country.

Minor villains aid and abet the scurrilous schemes of the major looters and moochers, some actively, some inadvertently. Rand uses these minor characters to illustrate the pervasiveness of the effects of the whim-worshiping society. Like a plague, collectivism, altruism, and mysticism spread their poisonous effects throughout the culture. In a society in control of the nonproductive and irresponsible, disaster is bred. This is tellingly illustrated by the Comet tunnel disaster.

In her notes about writing this section of the novel, Rand explains that the disaster is made possible by the fact that though times have changed, people rely on the discipline and confidence created by the old morality of rationality and good performance. But once a society changes in such a way that need and pull are the measures of a person's ability to get and keep a job rather than objective performance, the purpose of a railroad, or any business, ceases to be. She concludes, "this is all the good that the seizure of material wealth, without the mind, will do for the looters" (*J,* 622).

The cast of characters for this Taggart Tunnel disaster is encompassing. It includes everyone from James Taggart, the president of the railroad, to a bewildered boy who runs the Teletype machine. In a society of pull where rules and regulations are not applied equally, everyone shifts the blame onto someone else. Taggart shifts the blame to Clifton Locey. "It's your job," Taggart says. Locey, who knows it is impossible, writes orders to David Mitchum to do the job "safely." Locey then disappears so that no one can ask him how. Mitchum, who is smart enough to know he is being set up to be the fall guy if an accident occurs, doesn't understand the connection between the manner of his getting this unearned job and his being framed. As Rand's narrator explains, they are "inextricable parts of a single whole" (*Atlas Shrugged,* 552). Mitchum tries to pass it off on Brent, who quits. The disillusioned train master and conductor, both able, but with reasons not to care anymore, allow the disaster to go forward. Add to the mix Joe Scott, a drunk who got his job because of friendship, and Luke Beal, a fireman who thinks his superiors know what they are doing, and there is no way that the disaster could be prevented. Those who could either quit or don't care. Those left in charge are incompetent and refuse to take responsibility.

Lest the hapless passengers on this doomed train evoke our sympathies, Rand gives us a catechism of their "sins." Her ironic descriptor for them in her journal is "the passengers 'who weren't guilty' " (*J*, 622). Then she catalogs their sins. Named are characters such as Kip Chalmers, a second-rate politician who makes the demands that propel the train into the disaster. Laura Bradford is his mistress, a movie star who sleeps her way to the top through bureaucratic ranks. Gilbert Keith-Worthing is the flabby and obese British novelist who claims there is no such thing as freedom, and Lester Tuck is an attorney who used to represent shoplifters.

Among the unnamed passengers are a sociology professor who teaches that it is the masses who count, not the individual, and a journalist who believes that good causes justify the use of force but isn't quite clear about what defines a good cause. A teacher who has taught generations of students to bow to the will of the majority and a newspaper publisher who believes that men are evil by nature and therefore unfit to be free are also on the train.

The Taggart anniversary dinner is another gathering of the repugnant and repulsive. In total disregard for her husband's feelings, Lillian invites people he disdains and even people who have attacked him publicly. No one invited is Hank Rearden's friend, though admittedly the narration does not give the reader reason to believe that he has any. Lillian Rearden's unnatural allies are her mother-in-law and brother-in-law. Mrs. Rearden, Hank's mother, is a nagging, critical, reproachful woman who only knows how to take. And though her son is her sole support, she still complains that he does not pay enough attention to her and his brother, giving them only money and none of his time. Still, she has no idea what his interests are, reproving him for missing dinner on the day he has poured the first sample of his great invention. She does not appreciate her son's abilities and seeks to keep him bound by guilt. Like his mother, Philip Rearden depends totally on his brother's largesse. But rather than appreciating Hank's charity, Philip Rearden lives in Hank's home and criticizes him. A sickly, tired man, affected with a chronic weariness though the doctor can find no cause for his precarious health, Philip works for organizations that oppose his brother's work, committing the effrontery of asking Hank for money while not letting the source of the money be known. Eventually Philip spies on his brother for the government.

Lillian's invitees to the party are an assortment of mouthpieces for ideas and attributes Rand abhors, among them altruism, mysticism, irrationality, and worship of the zero. Mouthing the premises of naturalism and postmodernism, Balph Eubank is the literary leader of the period. He espouses the critical view that "plot is a primitive vulgarity in literature" (129). Because he believes that the essence of life is defeat and suffering, for him that is what literature should portray. In choosing the name Balph, Rand expresses her contempt for affected names. Balph espouses views that would make Rand regurgitate, which may account for the onomatopoeic closeness of his name to the word "barf." Other guests include Dr. Simon Pritchett, the author of *The Metaphysical Contradictions of the Universe,* a book that promotes the thesis that human beings are just chemistry and biology and everything is a matter of opinion. His premise is that "logic is a primitive vulgarity of philosophy" (129). A prime moocher in the group is

Mort Liddy, a composer of old-fashioned movie scores. Lacking his own creative ability, Liddy popularizes and mangles a Richard Halley concerto to win an award for best movie score of the year. Claude Slagenhop is moocher, looter, and altruist. The only right he recognizes is need, proclaiming that because there are hungry people, there should be the right to seize the means of production. He is president of Friends for Global Progress. The name Slagenhop suggests nothing so much as slag heap. A collectivist through and through, he thinks that there is no source for public opinion, only the collective instinct of the collective mind.

That Bertram Scudder would be at the party is indicative of Lillian Rearden's desire to hurt her husband. Bertram Scudder is the editor of *The Future* magazine, in which he writes nasty articles about Hank Rearden. Later in the plot, Scudder is the broadcaster on the radio program Dagny appropriates to denounce the government for their blackmailing of Hank Rearden. His tone is an attempt to sound "cynical, skeptical, superior, and hysterical together" (783). Among the other miserable nonentities who espouse amorality or immorality are characters such as Betty Pope, a member of one of the "best families," who sleeps with Jim Taggart. Even their sexual relations are characterized in an unappealing manner. She is homely, slovenly, and passionless.

Rand's minor villains are fat, loud, uncouth, and generally unappealing. None is independently productive. They wheedle, they whine. If they make money, it is through government favors. If they achieve position, it is through pull and influence, not ability. Dr. Blodgett is a young, fattish scientist who pulls the lever to demonstrate Project X. Orren Boyle is large, loud, and has slitlike eyes. Tinky Holloway is rat faced, slim, and slouching. Lee Hunsacker looks worn-out at age 42; he is a whiner who blames everyone but himself for his failures. Ben Nealy is soft, bulky, and sullen. Even Mr. Thompson, the Head of State, is a nondescript, wilted-looking man.

It falls to Cuffy Meigs, an ignorant, uncouth lout of bulging girth and nasal voice, to create the most destruction. He takes over Project X and drunkenly and stupidly pulls the wrong lever on the xylophone, devastating everything within a hundred-mile radius.

The most refreshing of these minor villains is Fred Kinnan, a racketeer who heads Amalgamated Labor of America. Kinnan, at least, is one of the most honest of the looters. He does not pretend that he is doing anything else. He calls the actions of the government an "anti-industrial revolution" (504) and points out the pitfalls of their actions or lack of action. Ayn Rand used the phrase again in the title of her 1971 anthology *The New Left: An Anti-Industrial Revolution*.

6

Themes

Ayn Rand's early journal entries for *Atlas Shrugged* show that she began making notes for a novel about the mind on strike in early 1945, although she had thought about the basic plot and theme more than a year earlier. The novel's working title at that point was *The Strike*. It was not renamed until 1956, when her husband, Frank O'Connor, suggested that *Atlas Shrugged* would make a good title for the novel. Until then "Atlas Shrugged" had been simply a chapter title. Rand's initial purpose for the novel was to show why the mind is important in the political-economic realm, what would happen to the world if the men and women of the mind went on strike. Of course, the work grew in scope as she got further into her project (*J*, 389). It is hard to believe now that in that original planning stage, Rand had expected the novel to be a briefer work than *The Fountainhead*. The difference in length between her original projection and the extant novel provides sufficient page count for a good-sized novel. Her first work, *We the Living*, is about that number of pages.

Rand's journal notes indicate that as she worked through preliminary planning, particularly in her thinking about how *Atlas Shrugged* would be different from *The Fountainhead,* she decided that *Atlas Shrugged* would be more social, with an enlarged scope beyond the lives of a few characters. *The Fountainhead* is a novel that focuses on a personal story, a novel in which the theme of individualism is pervasive. The plotline charts the rise of one heroic and individualistic architect, Howard Roark, as he builds his career among derivative colleagues and second-handers. The novel begins and ends with him. His triumph is charted in the final part, a part that bears his name.[38] The three other major sections of the novel also bear the names of characters, three other men in the novel whose destinies are inextricably linked with Roark's. Although Howard Roark wins his battles, and the climactic scene is his exoneration at a trial that establishes his rights of contract, there is little sense that the society as a whole is much affected.

Atlas Shrugged, on the other hand, concerns itself not only with certain individual struggles but with the impact of those struggles on the governance of the United States and the world. This larger scope necessitates the introduction of numerous themes, both great and small, on subjects of individual and societal import. The novel is divided into three parts; its chapter and part titles are generally keys to the philosophical or thematic concepts Rand is exploring, such as "the aristocracy of pull," "the sanction of the victim," or "the sign of the dollar." Of key importance is Rand's plan to illustrate the integration and admixture among our personal and public beliefs, the underlying interconnections among such areas as mind and body, individual and society, economics and ethics.

One place to begin discussion of Rand's major themes is with the selections from *Atlas Shrugged* she chose to reprint in *For the New Intellectual: The Philosophy of Ayn Rand.* Published in 1961, *For the New Intellectual* is the first book by Rand to appear after the publication of *Atlas Shrugged* and marked her introduction as a public philosopher. In it are a lengthy original essay, brief excerpts from her earlier works, and eight selections from *Atlas Shrugged.* These eight selections serve as convenient encapsulations or précis of the preponderance of Rand's themes.

"The Meaning of Money"

At the Rearden anniversary party, Bertram Scudder, one of Rand's sleazier villains, remarks to a woman, in his effort to discount Francisco d'Anconia's statement that the world will get exactly what it deserves: "Don't let him disturb you. You know, money is the root of all evil—and he is the typical product of money" (382). Scudder's evocation of this banal aphorism, so often and easily repeated, provides Rand with the opportunity to turn the concept on its head. Francisco d'Anconia, as Rand's mouthpiece, presents a contrary argument. He delivers a "money is the root of all good" rebuttal.

Francisco begins by defining money as "the material shape of the principle that men who wish to deal with one another must deal by trade and give value for value" (382). In the development of this theme, he points out that money is a tool of exchange, a tool that facilitates trade. In one of her later works, Rand would enlarge on this definition, pointing out that money is not only a tool of exchange but also a tool of saving. Money allows one to store or delay the result of the exchange for future use. Money is also a symbol of trust, for to accept a piece of paper, you must believe that there is financial backing behind it that will not default on, or devalue, what that paper represents. As Francisco explains: "To trade by means of money is the code of the men of good will." On the other hand, he explains, "So long as men live together on earth and need means to deal with one another—their only substitute, if they abandon money, is the muzzle of a gun" (385). Still, though Francisco makes a generic defense of money in this speech, in Galt's Gulch, the ideal republic of the novel, there is no paper money, but only gold and silver coin. This is because gold and silver represent objective value. In this Rand harks back to earlier times when coins were made of precious metals. Paper money, too, was a certificate for an equivalent value in gold or silver. Rand's last speech was to the National Committee for Monetary Reform, an organization that seeks to reestablish the gold standard and educate United States citizens about the benefits of a free market economy.

For Rand there is a clear connection between money and morality. In her journal notes for Francisco's speech, she writes: "Another proof of the noble nature of money is that people are able to keep it only so long as they keep their virtues—and no longer" (*J*, 596). In Rand's reasoning, when people become corrupt or careless, a swarm of looters will find a way to seize their money. Examples include the number of heirs who either have been wrecked by not having to earn their money or have lost all the money they inherited. Francisco explains, "If an heir is equal to his money, it serves him; if not, it destroys him" (*Atlas Shrugged*, 384). People must live up to their money, and to do so they must have respect for it. Rand's premise is that for a man to respect money, he has to have earned it. On the converse, people who have obtained money dishonorably are people who can easily disdain it.

In Rand's hierarchy of values, money is the product of virtue. That virtue consists of the ability to make money by dint of one's own efforts. The person who loves money loves its nature. "To love money is to know and love the fact that money is the creation of the best power within you. ... The lovers of money are willing to work for it. They know they are able to deserve it" (384). Still, she points out, there is much money cannot do. It cannot buy happiness, intelligence, admiration, or respect. Cheats and frauds and parasites are attracted to the fool who thinks it can.

Connected with her theme of the positive value of money is her admiration for the United States as a country of money. The dollar sign, which she uses as a primary symbol in the novel, is a combination of the initials *U* and *S*, and she explains that the United States is the country that originated the concept of "making" money. She calls America the country of money, the country of the self-made man, where aristocracy is based on wealth rather than on blood. In choosing the dollar sign as a symbol, Rand is again using one of her most effective thematic tools, that of taking a term or idea that is generally considered negatively and redefining it.[39] When Dagny Taggart asks Owen Kellogg what the dollar sign means, he responds that typically it has been emblazoned on the vest of every cartoon piglike figure that stands for a crook, grafter, or scoundrel. Instead, Kellogg explains, the dollar sign stands for the money of a free country, where the earning of it means achievement, success, and ability. Rather than serving as a mark of condemnation, it should be a mark of pride. In Kellogg's opinion, the United States is the only country in history "where wealth was not acquired by looting, but by production, not by force, but by trade, the only country whose money was the symbol of a man's right to his own mind, to his work, to his life, to his happiness, to himself" (*Atlas Shrugged*, 630).

THE MARTYRDOM OF THE INDUSTRIALISTS

The title imagery of the novel is embedded in the scene that produces the theme of the martyrdom of the industrialists. The scene takes place in Hank Rearden's factory. In a long presentation to Hank Rearden, Francisco d'Anconia offers his explication of how industrialists hold up the world. Then he asks Hank Rearden what he would tell Atlas to do if he saw him holding up the world, "blood running down his chest, his knees buckling, his arms trembling but still trying to hold the world aloft with the last of this strength, and the greater his effort the heavier the world bore down on his shoulders" (424). Rearden responds that he does not know and asks d'Anconia what he would tell him. D'Anconia answers, "To shrug."

The context for this scene is that Ken Danagger, one of Rearden's closest business associates, has just decided to quit and abandon his coal mines. The reader understands later in the novel that John Galt has convinced Danagger to join the strike and that this is d'Anconia's attempt to communicate to Rearden the same message. However, Francisco does not get to finish this presentation because they are interrupted by an emergency in Rearden's mills.

Some of the message, however, is communicated before they are interrupted and provides a moral justification for capitalism. Francisco begins by telling Hank that he is one of the last moral men left to the world. When Hank asks him why he says that, Francisco points to the mills and says, "If you want to see an abstract principle, such as moral action, in material form—there it is" (420).

Francisco leads Hank through a series of questions to make him understand that he has accepted a wrong moral code. As basis for his argument, Francisco explains that every girder, pipe, and valve in the mills had to be chosen by Rearden, using his best judgment, to accomplish his purpose, the making of his steel. More than that, he has spent 10 years of his life developing Rearden Metal with the expectation of making money from exchanging his best effort in making the best rail ever made for the best effort of others. When Francisco asks Hank if he has made money and gotten appreciation for what he has done, Rearden answers that he has not. Instead he has been condemned.

Francisco asks Hank for whom he made his metal. Did he create for the giants of productive energy who could think of creative and innovative ways to use it and the appreciative average people who would be thankful for the benefits of his labors? Rearden affirms that those are the users he had envisioned. Conversely, d'Anconia asks Rearden if he had worked incessantly for the whining rotters who never create anything but still demand that others pay their way. He asks Rearden if he would be proud to serve people who think that their need is a higher claim to reward than his effort, people who sneer and curse the very geniuses whose products they are using, whose products make their lives easier.

What d'Anconia wants Rearden to reevaluate is whether he is putting his talents at the service of evil and letting it be used as a tool for the destruction of what he values. And as Rearden listens, the words that come to his mind are "the sanction of the victim." D'Anconia further clarifies Rearden's situation and the situation of all productive industrialists who find themselves denounced not for their faults but for their achievements. D'Anconia notes that they are called cruel for their unyielding integrity, arrogant for their independent minds, antisocial for their daring to venture down undiscovered roads, ruthless for their strength and self-discipline, greedy for their power to create wealth. In his defense of industrialists such as Rearden, d'Anconia explains that they have been called parasites, robbers, and exploiters when it is they who have expended the energy, created the abundance, and kept people alive through their production.

Francisco tells Hank that he has accepted the moral code of his inferiors and has given them a weapon with which to enslave him. His greatest guilt is accepting the undeserved guilt they have heaped upon him. It is Hank's virtue, in the form of his ability to create and produce, that keeps the nonproductive alive. But although it is they who need him and not he who needs them, he has allowed them to use that need and impotence as justification for his immolation, for adding to his ever increasing burden. It follows, then, that he is the Atlas who needs to shrug.

⁃The Moral Meaning of Capitalism

Rand is fond of courtroom scenes. Trials provide significant plot junctures in many of her works. Although it is a truism in the American justice system that one who acts as one's own lawyer has a fool for a client, in Rand's fictive world, the opposite is true. Howard Roark presents his own defense in *The Fountainhead,* and Hank Rearden presents his own case in *Atlas Shrugged.* His speech to the court amplifies several of Rand's significant messages. One particular argument has to do with questioning the premises underlying the concept that the good of the group is more important than the individual's rights. In any kind of collectivist state, the principle of the public good is primary. Rand believes, however, that this is based on a false logic, and she uses the trial of Hank Rearden as an occasion to make the argument.

Rearden is tried for ignoring government regulations about how much and to whom he can sell his metal. Invoking the principle of property rights, Rearden's basic defense is that he does not recognize the validity of a law that allows the disposal of his property without his consent or the court's right to try him. The judge tells Rearden that the law he is denouncing is based on the highest principle—the principle of the public good. Rearden's rejoinder is to go to the root of such a principle, and he counters the concept of "a public good" with some telling arguments. First, he asks, who is the public and who determines their good? Then he questions the difference between a public that would seize someone's goods because it determines it needs them and a burglar who does likewise. He explains that there are no conflicts of interest among people who do not demand the unearned. But if the public good is served by the sacrifice of one, then the violation of the rights of the one is ultimately the violation of the rights of all. No good can be achieved by making some people victims or by sacrificing some individuals for the benefit of others.

Rearden refuses to participate in a system that requires his consent; he refuses to give the system the appearance or veneer of justice. Therein lies one of Rand's insights into how the able and productive of the world are harnessed and kept in check by the weak. It is called "the sanction of the victim." It is a process by which a person's virtues are the weapons that are turned against him or her. The ability to do this rests on the emotion of guilt. Hank Rearden begins to understand it when he listens to his wife, Lillian, at their Thanksgiving dinner.

What Rearden comes to understand is that his own high sense of honor is necessary for her to heap dishonor on him. It is his sense of moral rectitude that allows her to accuse him of moral depravity. If he had no honor or moral rectitude, her accusations would mean nothing to him. It is his very virtues that she counts on to give her power over him. To feel guilty or ashamed, he had to accept her code of values. Once he has come to the conclusion that he does not value her judgment, she loses any power over him.

Rearden questions what kind of code requires the victim's own virtue to fuel it. He concludes that such a code would destroy only those who tried to observe it. It is a punishment from which only the honest would suffer. "Could one conceive of an infamy lower than to equate virtue with pain, to make virtue, not vice, the source and motive of power of suffering?" (432).

THE MEANING OF SEX

Rand develops her theme about the meaning of sex in several important plotlines.[40] The most essential and dramatic one is Hank Rearden's gradual reeducation through his love affair with Dagny Taggart. Although Hank Rearden is a heroic character, he has been so focused on his work that he has not had time to reflect on the nature of love and sex. Like many of Rand's generation, he has separated them. Therefore, initially, he feels guilty about his sexual desires for Dagny and thinks that her welcoming them somehow devalues her. That his response to a woman he has admired in the highest terms should be sexual is for him evil. Only in the course of his relationship with Dagny does he begin to learn otherwise.

In Rand's hierarchy of values, sex plays an important role. She does not subscribe to the mind-body dichotomy. For her, mind and body are inextricably linked. There is no "*essential,* unbreakable tie between sex and spirit—which is the tie between body and soul" (*J*, 609). She wrote that there was a time when people believed sex was inherently evil, that it needed the spiritual aspects of marriage to serve as a way of redeeming and excusing it, of making it a pardonable weakness. For her, when a man wants a woman, it is a great compliment. Therefore, she explained, a husband should feel honored if another man wants his wife. Such desire would be the expression of a natural and proper admiration. But, of course, the wife would not act on that desire, since exclusivity would be the material form of her love for her husband. By adhering to this philosophy, Galt is able to feel no jealousy, only "non-malicious" envy, about Dagny's affairs with Francisco and Hank Rearden. What he does not feel is that she has been demeaned or degraded in any way by these relationships.

Rand noted that since most people's philosophies were a "hodgepodge of contradictory bits," so was their attitude toward sex (*J*, 609). This does not mean that she endorsed sex without commitment. She also condemned such theories as free love, which she called silly, since it simply glorified physical joy while forgetting the moral and the spiritual.

In *Atlas Shrugged,* Rand has Francisco deliver a lengthy dissertation to Hank, one in which he explains that "a man's sexual choice is the result and the sum of his fundamental convictions" (*J*, 609). He argues that what a man finds sexually attractive, the type of women he chooses as a sexual partner, is reflective of his evaluation of himself.

Thus if a man chooses the highest type of woman, a woman he can admire, one who is strong and hard to conquer, then he is demonstrating his attraction to a woman who reflects his deepest vision of himself. A man of self-esteem chooses a heroine.

By contrast, Francisco explains, a man who is "convinced of his own worthlessness will be drawn to a woman he despises" (*Atlas Shrugged*, 455). Such a woman can give him a momentary illusion of his own value. However, only a man who despises himself can gain self-esteem from sexual adventures. For Rand, sex is not the cause but the effect of a man's sense of self. It is "the means for expressing in physical form one's greatest celebration of life, of joy, of one's highest self-exaltation and one's highest moral values" (*J,* 606).

"Love is our response to our highest values," Francisco declares.

> Let a man corrupt his values and his view of existence, let him profess that love is not self-enjoyment but self-denial, that virtue consists, not of pride, but of pity or pain or weakness or sacrifice, that the noblest love is born, not of admiration, but of charity, not in response to *values,* but in response to *flaws*—and he will cut himself in two. (*Atlas Shrugged,* 456)

People who damn existence as evil are attracted to evil. If one feels damned, then depravity is what will attract. Only the man who claims that love is divorced from desire is capable of the "depravity of desire devoid of love."

In the plot of the novel, it is important for Rearden to understand how he has been victim to the mind-body dichotomy, how he has accepted a false divide between the mental and the physical. In Rand's perception, such a false divide makes people into creatures cut in half, swinging desperately between one side and the other. When people do not have integrated values, when they despise the physical and the material (which includes money, skyscrapers, and factories) and subscribe instead to some indefinable concept of a spiritual meaning of life and virtue at odds with the body, then relationships result in disasters. This mind-body split creates a situation whereby a man will be unable to desire the woman he loves, but will be unable to resist a "brainless slut."

Because of this evaluation of human sexuality as a celebration of life, an expression of self-esteem, and the highest possible integration of mind and body, Thomas Gramstad finds Rand's view to be essentially pagan and Aristotelian. He calls it "a secular reformulation of the pagan rite known as 'the Sacred Marriage of God and Goddess, the defining characteristic of which is the 'reunion of nature and spirit.' "[41]

FROM EACH ACCORDING TO HIS ABILITY, TO EACH ACCORDING TO HIS NEED

Dagny Taggart learns the story of Twentieth Century Motor Company from Jeff Allen, the bum she invites to be a guest in her railroad car. He worries that he and the workers at the company may have started the expression "Who is John Galt?" Allen tells her that the man who said he would put an end to the Marxist concept that destroyed Twentieth Century was named John Galt. But before Allen gives her Galt's name, he recounts for her the story of how a profitable company was ruined by the heirs who decide to run it according to the communist credo. The plan was that all employees in the factory would work according to their abilities but would be paid according to their needs. Allen believed at first that workers voted for the plan because they thought it was good or thought they should think it was good. In the course of the experience, he comes to a different conclusion:

> There wasn't a man voting for it who didn't think that under a setup of this kind he'd muscle in on the profits of the men abler than himself. There wasn't a man rich or smart enough but that he didn't think that somebody was richer and smarter and this plan would give him a share of his better's wealth and brain. (*Atlas Shrugged*, 616)

The devil, of course, is in the details. How are need and ability established? To determine need and ability, the entire group votes. The result turns the workers into beggars because they have to prove their need to their fellows. Each becomes a panhandler, claiming his need is worse than his neighbor's. Ability is also voted on, so people begin to hide their abilities so that they will not be assigned more work than their fellows. When the productive find that rather than being rewarded for their ideas and abilities, they are assigned more work, they quit offering ideas and slow down.

Allen recalls that competition in the profit system had been called vicious. But he explains that there is nothing more vicious than the competition to do poorly, not to display ability. There is nothing more destructive than forcing a person to do *not* his or her best but the worst possible job. There is nothing more detrimental for self-esteem. When people see that their efforts have no palpable rewards, then why expend the effort? Working ceases. In a parallel manner, if a person's efforts all go not to one's own welfare but to fulfilling the needs of the less fortunate, then the needy become not the object of concern but the objects of resentment.

The result of such a situation is that those who truly believed in the morality of the premise of "from each according to his ability, to each according to his need," are the ones punished most. They are the ones who continue working hard even as they get less than those who do little. It is a system in which those who cheat get the biggest rewards. Honesty is punished, dishonesty rewarded. Allen sums up the situation:

> What was it we were supposed to want to work for? For the love of our brothers? What brothers? For the bums, the loafers, the moochers we saw all around us? And whether they were cheating or plain incompetent, whether they were unwilling or unable— what difference did that make to us? ... Love our brothers? That's when we learned to hate our brothers for the first time in our lives. (613–14)

In such a society, normally happy occurrences turn sour. Because marriage and children create more mouths to feed, rather than celebrate these events at Twentieth Century Motors, they became the source of resentment for those who will have to produce more or share what they have with more people.

Naturally, the able and the competent are the first to leave such a system. When this happened, then the quality of the product deteriorated, and business fell off. Customers do not place orders because a factory "needs" orders. Need does not power generators or operate machinery without electricity or keep an airplane flying. What Allen does not understand is how so many leading thinkers, leaders, and professors could ever make the mistake of not understanding how faulty and illogical the communist credo is.

Rand's antipathy to communism came from firsthand experience and lasted her lifetime. She began her anticommunist theme in her first published novel, *We the Living,* but develops it more thoroughly in *Atlas Shrugged.* Rand challenges the very tenets of Marxist thinking. Basic to Marx is his claim that the collectivity of man is the human essence and that one should live through and for humanity, not for one's own welfare or excellence. Although Marx names his eventual goal as individual emancipation and fulfillment, his future society will be one constituted by citizens who renounce their own happiness in favor of collective welfare.

Writing when she did, Rand had to create a fictional company to illustrate how the communist credo would work in a real-life situation. She did not live to see the failure of communist economic systems worldwide. One wonders what she would have thought about President Mikhail Gorbachev proclaiming, in his analysis of the flaws in the economic system of the USSR, that the Soviet worker had forgotten how to work. Even the vast labor pools of Communist China have not precluded the necessity to create capitalist enterprise zones.

THE FORGOTTEN MEN OF SOCIALIZED MEDICINE

At a dinner in Mulligan's Valley, Dr. Hendricks explains to Dagny why he quit practicing medicine and dropped out. It happened when medicine was put under state control. What Hendricks argues is that after years of study, the development of skills that take years of passionate, merciless, excruciating devotion to acquire, he was not going to put his talents and abilities at the service of people whose sole qualification was their ability to get elected. Why should a bureaucrat make a medical decision? Hendricks questions why all the talk about health care revolves around the needs of the patients, with no attention paid to the needs of the doctor. In Hendricks's opinion, a man who would allow himself to be so enslaved is too dangerous to be entrusted with the care of patients. "Let them discover the kind of doctors that their system will produce. Let them discover, in their operating rooms and hospital wards, that it is not safe to place their lives in the hands of a man whose life they have throttled" (687).

THE NATURE OF AN ARTIST

Like Dr. Hendricks, who represents the position of the medical profession to Dagny, Richard Halley speaks for the artist. In the plotline, Halley had quit at the moment of his greatest success. He explains to Dagny that he did so because he could not accept the attitude of his audience that his suffering during all the years when he was struggling to reach his goal had been their due. He is appalled by the implication that an artist owes his audience any amount of struggle, suffering, bearing, and acceptance of their sneers, contempt, and torture to teach them to accept his work. He rejects the idea that it is his proper purpose to teach, and that they have no parallel responsibility. This he sees as placing the audience in the category of looters of the spirit.

In her journals, Rand also discusses the false dichotomy between art and entertainment. She questions the common idea that art is serious and dull, while entertainment is empty and stupid, but enjoyable. She maintains that this is a result of an altruistic morality that equates the good with the painful and the enjoyable with the sinful. The public does not buy into this morality, she claims, and in her case, she may be right. Her works are both serious and popular.

THIS IS JOHN GALT SPEAKING

John Galt's speech is the thematic climax of the novel.[42] Although many of the ideas incorporated in Galt's treatise have been presented earlier in partial form by different characters, they serve mainly to prepare the reader for this speech. It is in John Galt's address to the nation that the position of the strikers is thoroughly explicated, particularly in terms of its moral implications.

Given the number of other philosophical speeches that precede it, there has been some debate about the necessity for this pamphlet-length dissertation that runs from page 928 to page 984 of the novel. In response, it can be argued that because Rand's description of the maladies that infect the world has been so copiously illustrated, it is not unfitting that her diagnosis and prescription should be provided in a detailed and protracted form.

Up until the time of the speech, readers have been given bits of information, limited explanations. They know that the producers in society are vanishing, withdrawing their productive capabilities. The reader has waited impatiently with Dagny, outside the door, as "the destroyer" convinces yet another producer to quit. Dagny's wait is about three hours, so we know that the argument is a lengthy one. Components of the major themes, as articulated in the earlier speeches, have also been presented throughout the novel. At one point, Francisco d'Anconia begins to present the argument to Hank Rearden (his speech goes on for five pages), but they are interrupted by an accident at Rearden Mills. Some 500 pages later, d'Anconia resumes the argument: "Now I'll tell you things I had come to say, but did not finish, that night when I came here the first time" (*Atlas Shrugged*, 919). This time, however, the reader is not made privy to Francisco's speech. However, Galt's appropriation of the airwaves for his climactic presentation follows shortly. In it he explains, "If you wish to know . . . what I told them to make them quit, you are hearing it now" (933). He then presents all the pieces of the puzzle, the rationale behind the strike of the mind.

It is a carefully considered and meticulously argued philosophical rationale for the morality of the producers of the world. His presentation explains why the world finds itself in the crisis it is in, how human beings ought to act, and how political communities ought to be organized. He refutes the prevalent moralities, illustrating the harms they have caused. Rand's contention is that the maladies from which the world suffers are complex and deeply rooted in our most cherished institutions. The diagnosis and prescription are the purpose of Galt's speech.

The speech can be divided into four sections. First there is a brief introduction, then Galt presents the moral argument that underlies his position. Then he considers alternative moralities, or the argument between the producers' morality and that of their opponents. An analysis of how the moral truth explained in the earlier sections should be reflected in action concludes the speech.

The plot situation as Galt's listeners absorb his speech is that the world has been brought to a critical juncture. Production has dried up to the point where it is not the quality of life that is in danger but life itself. All the directives and government intervention have not improved the situation. Galt explains that the world crisis has come about because of a disagreement about moral questions. The strikers reject the popular understanding of good and evil.

Galt then analyzes the underlying differences in the definitions of good and evil that have brought about this moral crisis. The cause of the crisis, according to the morality preached by the political leaders, is that the producers are selfish profit seekers. If this is so, Galt explains, he has encouraged these profit seekers, these exemplars of evil, to remove themselves from society. With this evil removed, the world should then be good. Why, he asks, isn't it?

To understand the good, one must first establish certain essential principles. Galt begins by naming the "fundamental alternatives in the universe: existence or non-existence" (931). In human beings, he explains, there is not an instinct for self-preservation: "A desire is not an instinct" (931). And desire alone is not enough. There is a difference between having a desire and having the desire fulfilled, for unlike animals, which behave from instinct, human beings must choose how to act. Human beings are creatures of volitional consciousness. They must use their reason to choose those behaviors that will result in their survival. The choices one makes, then, can be judged accordingly: those that bring "that which is proper to the life of a rational being" are good, and those that harm it are evil (932). Human life serves as the standard of morality, and one's own life is its purpose.

How, then, does one make choices that will ensure a life proper to humans—choices whose purpose is "preserving, fulfilling, and enjoying the irreplaceable value which is one's life" (931)? Galt's answer is that one must understand that existence exists. It is the key axiom to the entire argument of Galt's speech. This implies both the end and the means of moral action, for as life (existence) is, so the first and fundamental goal of human beings is to preserve their existence as human beings. And the means by which to do this is human reason. To accept the axiom that existence exists is also to assume a conscious subject to perceive that something exists. That conscious being must identify the something that exists, and reason is the tool for doing so.

Reason operates according to a rule, the law of identity, "A is A." Logic applied to experience allows human beings to identify the facts of reality in a noncontradictory fashion. It is on these two basic premises, that things exist, and that human beings are able to understand that particular things exist because they are rational beings, that Galt builds a morality.

How then does one identify what is good, wherein lies virtue? Virtuous actions achieve valuable things. Because the goal is life, human existence, people should choose those values that enhance it. The supreme and ruling values, according to Galt, are reason, purpose, and self-esteem. Reason, because it is the means by which one acquires the knowledge needed to live, purpose because it provides a goal for reason to achieve, and self-esteem because with it human beings believe themselves worthy of life and able to achieve it. If reason, purpose, and self-esteem are the values, then the virtues are those things that promote those values.

Galt then enumerates and explains the virtues. Rationality is the recognition that the mind is the tool for guidance and judgment. Productiveness is acquiring knowledge and shaping matter to fit one's own purpose. Pride is realizing that one is one's own highest value. Independence is refusing to use the mind of another in place of one's own. Integrity is living according to one's convictions born of rationality. Honesty is refusing to accept anything unreal or irrational as valuable. Justice is evaluating and treating others according to what reason shows to be their real worth.

The virtue most immediate in the context of the speech is the question of justice in the dispute between the strikers and their fellow countrymen, for justice is the virtue of treating others well. And it is in this context that Galt develops his argument about how virtuous human beings ought to deal with one another. His premise is that people must deal with one another voluntarily in a trading situation where the self-interest of each is served.

Once Galt has defined the good, then the next question is about the nature of evil. The one act of evil that no person may commit is the initiation of physical force against another. This is because the use of force negates rationality. Force makes human beings do things that their reason tells them are against their self-interest. The use of force can be justified only in defense of oneself against another who has initiated the use of force, for that is the defense of the human and the rational against the nonhuman and irrational.

Once Galt has developed this metaphysical foundation for his moral beliefs, he is ready to compare the moral code of the strikers with the code of the moochers and looters who are in control of the government and society. He makes that comparison on several levels, the first of which is on the basis of results. In a world where producers are allowed to act according to their material beliefs, everyone benefits from the resultant products and development. However, it is not just the material that concerns Galt. The more basic philosophical argument concerns the battle between claimants on one's life, between what Galt identifies as those who claim your life belongs to God and those to claim it belongs to your neighbors. This choice, he explains, is between those who have preached self-sacrifice for the sake of ghosts in heaven and those who have preached self-sacrifice for the sake of incompetents on earth. He sees these as false alternatives. He notes, "And no one came to say that your life belongs to you and the good is to live it" (930).

Galt calls the two opposing forces, which he says are fundamentally similar as moralities, "mystics of the spirit" and "mystics of the muscle." In the introduction to *For the New Intellectual,* Rand personifies these two forces as the Witch Doctor and Attila, and her message is that both forces work against the progress of humans toward personal happiness. Both are "mystics" because both moralities are based on a rejection of the fundamental premise of rational proof, that A is A. Both reject the axiom that existence exists. Both put forth a "Morality of Death."

Galt defines the mystics of the spirit as those who reject reason in behalf of allegedly divine revelation. In the teachings of these mystics, humans are naturally evil, born with "original sin" or a natural tendency to evil that originates in the body. In this way of thinking, the body and consciousness are two enemies engaged in combat. They are

> two antagonists of opposite natures, contradictory claims, incompatible needs, that to benefit one is to injure the other, that his soul belongs to a supernatural realm, but his body is an evil prison holding it in bondage to this earth, and that the good is to defeat this body. (943)

The mystics of the spirit insist that true existence is consciousness and that the physical is neither essential to, nor good for, human life, that the body and the things that serve it are evil forces that seek to corrupt what is essentially human.

Galt derides the mystics of the spirit who claim they have a knowledge that transcends reason, that they have a special pipeline to some other world power. By claiming special knowledge that others supposedly lack, the mystics of the spirit are running a "protection racket" (955). They use the threat of eternal damnation to make human life miserable by branding all the virtues as vices. In that way they denigrate virtues such as pride, independence, rationality, and productiveness that are necessary to make humans happy and secure.

Whereas the mystics of the spirit are spiritualists, the mystics of the muscle are materialists. Their argument is that there is no absolute knowledge, that one cannot know the truth about what is good; therefore, the good is whatever most people—that is, whatever society—

decides it is. The key to the materialists' argument is that concepts, axioms, ideas, and arguments have no objective validity, that human ideas are created by material circumstances, and that ideas do not control matter, but that matter controls ideas.

Galt explains that the materialists contradict themselves, since they exercise human consciousness in the very act of declaring all claims of rational truth to be delusions:

> "We know that we know nothing," they chatter, blanking out the fact that they are claiming Knowledge—"There are no absolutes," they chatter, blanking out the fact that they are uttering an absolute—"You cannot prove that you exist or that you're conscious," blanking out the fact that proof presupposes existence, consciousness and a complex chain of knowledge: the existence of something to know, of a consciousness to be able to know it, and of a knowledge that has learned to distinguish between such concepts as the proved and the unproved. (956)

According to Galt, then, both the mystics of the spirit and the mystics of muscle make arguments for their moralities that are fundamentally flawed. Both deny what must be true in order for them to attempt to make the denial.

Galt concludes that neither the spiritualists nor the materialists achieve true human happiness. Rejecting their fundamentally flawed theories, Galt enunciates an alternative model for how human beings should act and how political communities should be organized.

The speech is also rich with challenges to common misconceptions. In it Rand presents some stimulating ideas, ideas that provoke us to rethink certain ways of viewing and defining things. Some examples are (1) the impotence of evil, which is only able to succeed when the good serves it; (2) praising nonprofit ventures while damning the profit ventures that are necessary to sustain the nonprofits; (3) defining public welfare as the welfare of those who do not earn it, while those who do earn it are entitled to no welfare; (4) the evil of refusing to judge so as to escape responsibility, thereby ending up with much of the responsibility for the blood spilled in the world; (5) the folly of a compromise between good and evil, for in such a compromise, evil always wins.

In sum, Galt proclaims the achievement of one's happiness as the *moral* purpose in one's life. In this, he is in keeping with the Declaration of Independence. His rationale for government, then, is that its purpose is to protect human rights, to create a society wherein life, liberty, and the pursuit of happiness are maximized. He states categorically:

> The only proper functions of a government are: the police, to protect you from criminals; the army, to protect you from foreign invaders; and the courts, to protect your property and contracts from breach or fraud by others, to settle disputes by rational rules, according to *objective* law. (977)

Antithetically, a government that initiates force against its neighbors or citizens is a bully who substitutes the law of "might makes right" for the law of reason.

The role of the mind is again emphasized toward the end of Galt's speech as he explains that every man who produces an idea, who discovers new knowledge, is a permanent benefactor of humanity (979). He explains that though material products are consumed by individuals and thus used up, the idea can be shared by all and continually reproduced.

Galt ends his speech by exhorting all citizens to join the strike, to refuse to allow the looters to continue using their abilities. He calls on them to be silent, not to volunteer, to vanish if possible. Then, when the looter state collapses, he promises that the strikers will return, with the dollar sign as their symbol, a sign of free minds and free markets, to rebuild the nation as it once was, a sanctuary for the rational being.

What Rand dramatizes in her novel is that the human mind is the fundamental survival tool humanity needs. One critic has gone so far as to identify the mind as the hero of *Atlas Shrugged,* calling the novel an ode, an epic poem in praise of intellectual achievement.[43] Rand does present a number of heroic people of the mind, and they serve as exemplars of her themes. In *Atlas Shrugged* these themes, taken together, serve as a manifesto of the mind.

VARIATIONS ON THE THEMES

Although most of Rand's messages are outlined in the eight major speeches summarized in the foregoing sections, there are variations on these and other themes throughout the novel. For example, the very idea of writing a novel about the mind on strike is unusual. Generally, when one thinks of a strike novel, one thinks of a novel where laborers refuse to labor. The cleverness of Rand's plot here is how she appropriates a traditionally socialist or Marxist theme and both refutes it and uses it to make her argument. In this novel, although there are laborers who refuse to work, it is the thinkers who refuse to think who cause the main problems in society. She takes the credo of "Workers of the world, unite. You have nothing to lose but your chains" and substitutes "thinkers" for "workers."

But though Rand stands the tradition of the strike novel on its head, making hers a novel of the rights of employers rather than the rights of employees, much of the thought content of her strike rationale echoes ideas developed earlier by both Henry David Thoreau and Dr. Martin Luther King Jr. In "On Civil Disobedience" Thoreau argues that when laws are unjust, just men belong in jail. Following Thoreau's lead, in his "Letter from Birmingham Jail," King makes the distinction between just laws and unjust laws, emphasizing the "moral responsibility to disobey unjust laws." In Rand's novel, the "strikers" also resolve not to obey unjust laws such as Directive 10-289, the Equalization of Opportunity Bill, and the Anti-dog-eat-dog Rule. But their course is not to go to jail. Instead they follow a course of passive resistance that was certainly a politically effective technique for Mahatma Gandhi in bringing Great Britain to the negotiation table and gaining independence for India. Martin Luther King Jr. also used the technique, perfected in the sit-in for his nonviolent movement. In effect,

Rand's strikers are following suit. They sit in by being in the world but not using their abilities to help motor it. Some drop out rather than sit in. Their methods are generally nonviolent, with notable exceptions such as the pirate activities of Danneskjöld and the dramatic rescue scene at the end when Francisco, Hank, Ragnar, and Dagny save John Galt from his torturers.

In earlier chapters, I have noted the number of times Rand employs the techniques of satirists, particularly irony, both dramatic and situational. Instead of a straightforward presentation of her ideas, either in the narrative or in the mouths of her spokesperson characters, she uses irony. She puts the ideas she finds abhorrent in the mouths of characters she finds repulsive, thereby underlining for the reader the wrongness of the ideas. In other words, she wants us to exercise our ironic ear and hear that we should oppose these ideas.

The occasion is a Thanksgiving dinner at Hank Rearden's home. Present are his wife, his mother, and his brother, all of whom he supports financially. The narrator describes the luxury of the surrounding, the cost of everything from the champagne to the table cloth. However, when the time comes for giving thanks, Hank's mother thanks God and Lillian for taking the trouble to make the dinner beautiful; his wife thanks the new cook; but no one thanks Hank, who pays the bills.

Challenging his purpose in defending himself in his upcoming trial, Lillian Rearden makes certain statements representative of the decadent culture she exemplifies. She calls Hank's thinking that he is right in his stance, conceit. "How do you know what is right?" she asks. "How can anyone know it? It is only a delusion to flatter your own ego and to hurt other people by flaunting your superiority over them" (431). Lillian goes further in her attempt to devalue Hank and his ability, in her attempt to make him see himself as no better than anyone else. She cautions him that the day of the hero is past. "Nobody is right or wrong, we're all in it together, we're all human— and the human is imperfect" (431). Barreling along in her recitation of repulsive bromides, she tells him to be practical, to "Live and let live. Give and take. Give in and take in" (431).

Mrs. Rearden, Hank's mother, is another of the despicable characters who mouth the ideas—or lack of ideas—that Rand finds abhorrent. When Rearden is about to go on trial for defying a government edict, his mother tells him he should cooperate with the government. When he asks her if she understands the issue in the case, she responds:

> No, I don't and I don't want to understand. It's all dirty business and dirty politics. All business is just dirty politics and all politics is just dirty business. I never did want to understand any of it. I don't care who's right or wrong, but what I think a man ought to think of first is his family. (434)

Her attitude is representative of a refusal to use the mind. She does not want to think about anything but her immediate needs. She does not care about the issues; she cares only that if Rearden is put in jail, her lifestyle may be affected.

Ragnar Danneskjöld is one of the novel's heroic figures, but Rand did not choose one of his speeches to reprint in *For the New Intellectual*. However, although he plays a lesser role in the plot than either Galt or d'Anconia, Rand does give Danneskjöld an important thematic function. In an encounter with Hank Rearden, replete with the ironic touches so characteristic of Rand, Danneskjöld explains to Rearden his anti–Robin Hood stance. Rand is an iconoclast if she is anything. Herein she takes on one of our culture's most cherished icons.

The scene is a dark and lonely road. Ragnar stops Rearden not to rob him but to give him gold. When Rearden questions the context of this action, Danneskjöld explains that when robbery is done in the daylight, sanctioned by law, then the only recourse for acts of honor or restitution is to go underground. Still, Rearden questions his methods, and so Danneskjöld explains that he has chosen the life of a pirate as his way of challenging the morality of the Robin Hood motif. His purpose, he explains, is to reverse what Robin Hood did. Robin Hood robbed from the rich and gave to the poor. He plans to rob from the thieving poor and give back to the productive rich. This he does by never attacking private ships or military vessels. Instead he seizes only those transports that carry the results of looting, such as subsidy ships, loan ships, relief ships, and "every vessel with a cargo of goods taken by force from some men for the unpaid, unearned benefit of others" (534). Although Ragnar acknowledges that Robin Hood had fought against looting rulers and returned the loot to those who had been robbed, that is not how the legend has been handed down.

> He is remembered, not as a champion of *property,* but as a champion of need, not as a defender of the robbed, but as a provider of the poor. He is held to be the first man who assumed a halo of virtue by practicing charity with wealth, which he did not own, by giving away goods, which he had not produced, by making others pay for the luxury of his pity. (534)

Moreover, Ragnar calls himself a policeman whose duty it is to protect citizens who are being robbed and return their goods to them. In this case, it is the government that is doing the robbing, and what Ragnar returns to Hank is gold in the amount of what Rearden has paid in income taxes for the last 12 years. Ragnar challenges the acceptance of death and taxes as the only certainties. He proclaims that humans should learn "to hold, not death and taxes, but life and production as their two absolutes and as the base of their moral code" (536).

Closely allied to Rand's theme of returning earnings to those who have a right to them is her celebration of work. In this novel, she tries to show how important it is that jobs be well done at every level of our society. Although her spotlight shines on high achievers, the inventors and industrialists, she does not forget the importance of everyone doing his or her job well. This she illustrates in a scene in Mulligan's Valley where Dagny encounters a young brakeman who becomes a grease monkey in the valley. Ellis Wyatt makes the statement that there is "no such thing as a lousy job—only lousy men who don't care to do it" (665). For Rand, the measure of human value is how well one does one's work, whatever that may be. The code of competence represents a gold-standard morality in Rand's assessment of productive and creative achievement.

Through all these thematic speeches and scenes, in all her characterization and plot turns, Rand returns to three main areas of conflict that must be resolved to create if not a utopian, at least an optimum, situation for human happiness and individual fulfillment. These antipodes are (1) individualism versus collectivism, (2) egoism versus altruism, and (3) reason versus mysticism. Collectivism, altruism, and mysticism are the "isms" that undermine human potential and set the world on the path to the dire future envisioned in *Atlas Shrugged*. Reason, egoism, and individualism are the routes to agency and productivity.

7

The Road to Hell

"The United States of America is the greatest, the noblest and, in its original founding principles, the *only* moral country in the history of the world." With this statement, Rand began the conclusion of her graduation address to the 1974 graduating class at West Point. She was a great patriot and appreciated the land of her choice, in the way that only one who grew up under tyranny can. In *The Ayn Rand Letter* she wrote that "America's founding ideal was the principle of individual rights ... [and that] everything 'noble and just,' and heroic and great, and unprecedented in human history—was the logical consequence of fidelity to that one principle." However, in *Atlas Shrugged* she creates a United States that looks little like a noble, just, and heroic country. What accounts for the deteriorated picture of our society?

One of Rand's most effective techniques is to demonstrate how people who may think they are operating by the most benign of intentions create the hell that plunges the world into a spiral of nonproductivity. Her special twist on the technique, however, is to demonstrate that in reality, often it is only a facade of good intentions. The underlying purpose of the people behind the smoke screen is power and greed for the unearned.

Three government directives are illustrative of how Rand employs this technique. They are the Equalization of Opportunity Bill, the Anti-dog-eat-dog Rule, and Directive 10-289. The National Alliance of Railroads passes the Anti-dog-eat-dog Rule. The alliance, which was formed putatively to protect the welfare of the industry, claims that by presenting a common front to the world, all the members will grow and prosper together. In the name of cooperation, members submit to the decisions of the majority, even if it is against their own interest. The claim of those who push the law is that the public welfare is being threatened by brutal dog-eat-dog competition (*Atlas Shrugged*, 76).

The reality behind this surface display of "good intentions" is illustrated in a scene between James Taggart, Orren Boyle, Wesley Mouch, and Paul Larkin. The four men talk the talk of unity and cooperation. Boyle says, "It's my absolute opinion that in our complex industrial society, no business enterprise can succeed without sharing the burden of the problems of other enterprises" (48). The truth behind this facade, however is that Boyle cannot deliver the rails he has promised, and rather than accept responsibility, he blames "conditions and circumstances absolutely beyond human control." "It's been proved that every business depends upon every other business. ... So everybody ought to share the burden of everybody else" (49). Boyle claims that his purposes is to preserve a free economy. He will not accept the responsibility for his failure, for in his way of thinking, success is attributed to luck. "It seems to me that the national policy ought to be aimed at the objective of giving everybody a chance at his fair share of iron ore, with a view toward the preservation of the industry as a whole" (50–51). Taggart chimes in: "You might ask yourself whether at a time of transportation shortages, when so many railroads are going bankrupt and large areas are left without rail service, whether it is in the public interest to tolerate wasteful duplication of services and the destructive dog-eat-dog competition of newcomers in territories where established companies have historical priority" (51). His underlying purpose is to prevent competition in productive areas where the customers want a better quality of service than he is able to deliver. The language may be about fairness and cooperation, but the purpose is running one's competitors out of business not because they cannot compete but because they do. For James Taggart, this accomplishes the death of the Phoenix-Durango Railroad, his chief competitor in Colorado.

The Equalization of Opportunity Bill is another bill couched in language of seemingly good intentions. The irony is that it depends on a rationale directly contrary to the Anti-dog-eat-dog edict. Whereas the one forbids competition, the other ensures it by not allowing any person or corporation to own more than one business concern. The looters and moochers of the culture want the bill to apply across the board. For example, Balph Eubank thinks it should apply to literature by restricting the sale of any one book to 10,000 copies so that other writers would have opportunities to sell their books. Bertram Scudder thinks that property rights should not be considered at all, that the people who own more than one business have their property only by courtesy of those who don't seize it. The rationale is that in times of reduced and dwindling production and markets, when it is so hard to make a living, the businesses that are doing well should be apportioned out to those who have not done well.

Directive 10-289 does not fit comfortably into the category of bills that are passed under the guise of "good intentions." The directive is obviously a response to a crisis situation. Because the looters and moochers are incompetent and cannot control the situation, they seek to freeze everything, to end any pretense of liberty. Of course, it does not work. Rand makes the argument, both literally and figuratively, that the more laws a government makes, the more freedom is destroyed and productivity curtailed.

The absorption of the mystic and altruistic mentality that Rand abhors by the citizens of this United States on the road to a collectivist hell is everywhere evidenced in the facile bromides that trip from their tongues. Refusal to judge or accept responsibility is excused by such expressions as "Who am I to ____? Say, do, decide." "It seems to me" and "in my opinion" preface all their statements, signaling their inability to make a judgment. Failure to act is excused with "The rules don't provide for it" (632). "We've done our best and nobody can blame us" is the mask for failure (48). Lack of principles is permitted because

"We can't go by rigid principles, we've got to be flexible, we've got to adjust to the reality of the day and act on the expediency of the moment" (339).

Looting the businesses of those who built them and earned their profits is licensed because profit is equated with selfish greed. On the other hand, businesses that don't make a profit are subsidized because the interest of society as a whole must always be placed first in any business undertaking (29). Businesses that serve the public are expected to work whether or not they make a profit (473).

Rand is particularly apt at demonstrating the perfidious nature of contemporary definitions of love as something irrational and sacrificial. For Lillian Rearden, the quality of love is defined not by any positive values but by the negation of the good. She claims that real devotion consists of being willing to lie, cheat, and fake to make another person happy (284). The corruption of values is her touchstone. If you tell an ugly woman she is beautiful, you offer her the greatest homage by corrupting the concept of beauty (285). "To love her for her vices is to defile all virtues for her sake—and that is a real tribute of love, because you sacrifice your conscience, your reason, your integrity and your invaluable self-esteem." "What's love ... if it's not self-sacrifice" (285).

James Taggart is another person who does not want to earn love by his virtues but wants unearned love and unearned greatness. He whines that he wants to be loved for himself, but not for his body, his works, or his actions. One is left to wonder what his definition of self is (813).

An Ending and a Beginning

More than 40 years have passed since the publication of *Atlas Shrugged*. For Rand, it marked both an ending and a beginning. It was the end of her career as a novelist. It was the beginning of her life as the leader of an intellectual movement and a public philosopher. It was a work that marked its author's life in a way that few works of fiction do. Its symbolism had become so inextricably linked with her life that at Ayn Rand's memorial service, there was a floral design in the shape of a dollar sign.

Atlas Shrugged was the last novelistic dramatization of Rand's philosophical premises. It served then as a springboard for their further elaboration and development. For the rest of her life, Rand wrote essays. In these essays, she continued to develop her aesthetic theories, her economic theses, her theory of epistemology. She wrote about ethics; she wrote about politics. Above all, she exhorted people to think, to check their premises, to develop integrated philosophies.

In the short afterword "About the Author" that follows *Atlas Shrugged,* Rand states, "My personal life is a postscript to my novels; it consists of the sentence: '*And I mean it.*' " The totality of Rand's fictional achievement in *Atlas Shrugged* is a manifesto of the mind. The rest of her career was spent proving that she meant it.

Notes and References

1. Quoted in Michael Paxton, *Ayn Rand: A Sense of Life* (Layton, Utah: Peregrine Smith, 1998), 18.

2. Barbara Branden, *The Passion of Ayn Rand* (New York: Doubleday, 1986), 14.

3. Chris Matthew Sciabarra has suggested that *Atlas Shrugged* is foreshadowed in a question posed by Howard Roark in *The Fountainhead:* "What would happen to the world without those who do, think, work, produce?" See Sciabarra, *Ayn Rand: The Russian Radical* (University Park: Pennsylvania State University Press, 1995), 402 n. 47.

4. The affair, which was kept secret from everyone except the involved spouses, was made public after Rand's death. Barbara Branden was the first to write of it in *The Passion of Ayn Rand*. Nathaniel Branden wrote of it both in *Judgment Day: My Years with Ayn Rand* and then in a revised version of that book, titled simply *My Years with Ayn Rand*.

5. Rand writes of this incident in "Introducing Objectivism," *Objectivist Newsletter* 1, no. 8 (August 1962): 35.

6. Jonathan Swift, *Gulliver's Travels and Other Writings*, ed. Louis A. Landa (Boston: Houghton Mifflin, 1960), 4.

7. "Brief Summary," *Objectivist*, September 1971, 1.

8. Ms. Rand was not persuaded. When I sent her a copy of the article and asked for an interview, the response was a letter from her lawyers threatening to sue me.

9. Ross Overbeek, "Rand-Bashing: Enough Is Enough," *Liberty* 1, no. 6 (July 1988): 56.

10. The Institute for Objectivist Studies changed its name to the Objectivist Center on 2 September 1999. One of its publication divisions is called the Atlas Society.

11. Joan Kennedy Taylor, E-mail message to author, 31 March 1999.

12. Quoted in Michael S. Berliner, ed., *Letters of Ayn Rand* (New York: Dutton, 1995), 7.

13. In "Prometheus," which was published in 1816, Byron hails Prometheus because he did "strengthen Man with his own mind," a sentiment much in keeping with Rand's themes in *Atlas Shrugged*. Mary Shelley writes of her husband's accomplishment in *Prometheus Unbound* that Shelley believed that "evil is not inherent in the system of creation," an idea that is in keeping with Galt's rebuke of the concept of Original Sin.

14. E-mail message to the author, 30 December 1999.

15. Ayn Rand's journal indicates that her choices of terms for the politicians and political system may have derived as much from her desire to convey her opinion of them as from her desire to project a future world. She writes: "Do not name their exact political positions. Keep it vague and general as it deserves. They are nonentities and their titles or jobs do not matter" (*J*, 453). Her choice of the name Mr. Thompson for the Head of State derives from her desire to make him undistinguished. She calls it the "anonymity of mediocrity."

16. Hans Gregory Schantz, <http://www.schantz.com/contents. htm#top>.

17. Branden writes of Rand's refusal to fly, which she rationalized as stemming from her distrust of the "modern psycho-epistemology of the mechanics and the pilots" (*PAR*, 318).

18. My thanks to David M. Brown for bringing this approach to my attention. Bryan Register made similar observations.

19. Still another interpretation is suggested by Bryan Register, who argues that *Atlas Shrugged* can be read as cyberpunk, a kind of postmodern science fiction. Cyberpunk is sometimes characterized by the overlapping of worlds formerly separate, such as the realm of high tech and the modern pop underground. It is a kind of hybridization, leveling the distinctions, among other things, between the technical and the literary, "high" and "popular" cultures. This generic flexibility is characteristic of a postmodern tendency to eradicate traditional categorical distinctions. Joseph Tabbi, in *Postmodern Sublime: Technology and American Writing from Mailer to Cyberpunk* (Ithaca, N.Y.: Cornell University Press, 1995), identifies the generic flexibility of cyberpunk as corresponding to "the sublime moment in both modernist and romantic literature. At least since Wordsworth the sublime has always 'brought the high and the low into dangerous proximity' " (211). Register points out that among the thematic concerns in *Atlas Shrugged* are the "breakdown of old modernist categories: theory/practice, fact/value, man/machine, and body/mind." He also notes that inasmuch as postmodern literature has something to do with chaos theory, Rand's work fits because she traces "the chaotic effects of unforeseen events" (undated letter to the author, 1999).

20. Nathaniel Branden, *My Years with Ayn Rand* (San Francisco: Jossey-Bass Publishers, 1999), 95.

21. Quoted by Leonard Peikoff in his introduction to the 35th anniversary edition of *Atlas Shrugged* (New York: Signet, 1992), 6.

22. Barbara Branden, *The Passion of Ayn Rand* (Garden City, N.Y.: Doubleday, 1986), 225. This is a more positive authorial projection of fantasy fulfillment than in any of her previous books. Although Kira is able and noble, she comes to a tragic end. Dominique is, in Rand's words, "myself in a bad mood."

23. Judith Wilt, "The Romances of Ayn Rand," in *Feminist Interpretations of Ayn Rand,* ed. Mimi Reisel Gladstein and Chris Matthew Sciabarra (University Park: Pennsylvania State University Press, 1999), 173.

24. Ibid.

25. Karen Michalson, "Who Is Dagny Taggart? The Epic Hero/ine in Diguise," in *Feminist Interpretations of Ayn Rand,* ed. Mimi Reisel Gladstein and Chris Matthew Sciabarra (University Park: Pennsylvania State University Press, 1999), 200.

26. We learned later that for a brief period, those legs belonged to Mary Tyler Moore.

27. Laura Mulvey, "Visual Pleasure and Narrative Cinema," *Screen* 16 (Autumn 1975): 6–18. Mulvey's influential article established the priority that classic American film gives to the male perspective, both narratively and visually.

28. A biographical sidelight that strengthens the identification of author and heroine is that Rand considered her legs her most attractive feature.

29. Wendy Martin, "Seduced and Abandoned in the New World: The Image of Woman in American Fiction," in *Woman in Sexist Society: Studies in Power and Powerlessness,* ed. Vivian Gornick and Barbara K. Moran (New York: New American Library, 1971), 329–46.

30. Although Dagny and Francisco are quite young when they consummate their love, he then remains celibate for a dozen years while he is pretending to be a playboy. Because he loses Dagny to John Galt, is one then to assume that Francisco will remain celibate for the rest of his life? Perhaps in Rand's fantasy that would be the correct response.

31. Edith de Rham, *The Love Fraud: A Direct Attack on the Staggering Waste of Education and Talent among American Women* (New York: Pegasus, 1965). De Rham's work argues that when women are convinced to devote their lives to love, a fraud is perpetuated that results in a staggering loss to the society.

32. Barbara Branden argues that both Dagny's and her creator's lives are "in most aspects . . . a feminist manifesto" ("Ayn Rand: The Reluctant Feminist," in *Feminist Interpretations of Ayn Rand,* ed. Mimi Reisel Gladstein and

Chris Matthew Sciabarra [University Park: Pennsylvania State University Press, 1999], 26).

33. Bryan Register thinks that because of "an unfortunate aspect of Rand's view of femininity," she subtly undercuts the feminist overtones of Dagny's character. He reads Dagny's delight in being John Galt's cook and housemaid—after the narrator has made it clear that Dagny thinks such activities are circular motion, whereas straight-line activities are "the badge of man"—as evidence that Rand's "implicit view is that women, as such, find their essential happiness in taking care of men, while men, as such, find their essential happiness in dealing with physical nature" (undated letter to author, 1999). His argument did not address the fact that when Dagny has the choice of staying in the valley with Galt or returning to her railroad, she chooses the latter. That she is not going to become a housewife, but will continue to run her railroads, is clear in the denouement when Hank Rearden says, "She will probably try to take the shirt off my back with the freight rates she's going to charge" (1073).

34. My thanks to Dr. Deane Mansfield-Kelley for suggesting the idea of an Arthurian archetype in *Atlas Shrugged*.

35. The numbers of literary contributions to the body of myth that is the Arthurian cycle is vast. Edward Donald Kennedy, in *King Arthur: A Casebook* (New York: Garland, 1996), xiv, cites more than 1,200 nineteenth- and twentieth-century works influenced by the myth. Therefore, it may be that the outlines of character and plot in my interpretation could differ from those of the reader. My reading is based mostly on the shared French and English tradition before the nineteenth- and twentieth-century revival.

36. Helen Beal Woodward, "Non-stop Daydream," *Saturday Review,* 12 October 1957, 25; Bruce Cook, "Ayn Rand: A Voice in the Wilderness," *Catholic World,* May 1965, 123; Robert Hunt, "Science Fiction for the Age of Inflation: Reading *Atlas Shrugged* in the 1980s," in *Coordinates: Placing Science Fiction and Fantasy, Alternative Series,* ed. George E. Slusser, Eric S. Rabkin, and Robert Scholes (Carbondale and Edwardsville: Southern Illinois University Press, 1984), 88; Nathaniel Branden, "The Literary Method of Ayn Rand," in *Who Is Ayn Rand?* (New York: Paperback Library, 1962), 81.

37. Thomas Gramstad, "The Female Hero: A Randian-Feminist Synthesis," in *Feminist Interpretations of Ayn Rand,* ed. Mimi Reisel Gladstein and Chris Matthew Sciabarra (University Park: Pennsylvania State University Press, 1999), 343.

38. Douglas J. Den Uyl argues for Dominque's centrality in the novel, noting that though there is not a section named for her, she pervades them all. See *"The Fountainhead": An American Novel* (New York: Twayne Publishers, 1999), 63.

39. Later she wrote two books in which she developed this technique further. *The Virtue of Selfishness* and *Capitalism: The Unknown Ideal.* There

is a brief discussion in Chris Matthew Sciabarra's *Ayn Rand: The Russian Radical,* 251–52.

40.   This discussion will be framed mostly in terms of men for two reasons. First, Rand herself used the masculine pronoun as the universal. Second, much of this discussion derives from a speech Francisco d'Anconia makes to Hank Rearden, in which he is talking in terms of men.

41.   Thomas Gramstad, "Self and Worship (Re: Who Is Dagny Taggart? Hero Worship)," *Randian-Feminism Internet Discussion List,* 8 July 1999, n.p.

42.   Robert Webking and I have published a fuller and more detailed analysis of John Galt's speech in "John Galt's Argument for Human Productivity in *Atlas Shrugged,*" *University of Windsor Review* (Windsor, Ontario) 21, no. 1 (1988): 73–83.

43.   Andrew Bernstein, *The Mind as Hero in "Atlas Shrugged,"* Second Renaissance Books, audiocassette.1994.

Selected Bibliography

Primary Works

Books

Anthem. London: Cassell and Company, 1938; rev. ed., Los Angeles: Pamphleteers, 1946; Caldwell, Idaho: Caxton Printers, 1953; paperback, New American Library, 1946; 50th anniversary edition, New York: Dutton, 1996.

Atlas Shrugged. New York: Random House, 1957; paperback, New York: New American Library, 1957; 35th anniversary edition, New York: Signet, 1992.

The Ayn Rand Column. Oceanside, Calif.: Second Renaissance Books, 1991.

The Ayn Rand Lexicon. Ed. Harry Binswanger. New York: New American Library, 1986.

Ayn Rand Marginalia. Ed. Robert Mayhew. New Milford, Conn.: Second Renaissance Books, 1995.

Capitalism: The Unknown Ideal. New York: New American Library, 1966; paperback, New York: New American Library, 1967.

The Early Ayn Rand: A Selection from Her Unpublished Fiction. Ed. Leonard Peikoff. New York: New American Library, 1983.

For the New Intellectual. New York: Random House, 1961; paperback, New York: New American Library, 1961.

The Fountainhead. New York: Bobbs-Merrill, 1943; paperback, New York: New American Library, 1952; 50th anniversary edition, New York: Bobbs-Merrill, 1993.

Introduction to Objectivist Epistemology. New York: New American Library, 1979. Paperback only.

Journals of Ayn Rand. Ed. David Harriman. New York: Dutton, 1997.

Letters of Ayn Rand. Ed. Michael S. Berliner. New York: Dutton, 1995.

The New Left: The Anti-industrial Revolution. New York: New American Library, 1971. Paperback only. *Return of the Primitive: The Anti-industrial Revolution.* Expanded edition with additional essays and introduction by Peter Schwartz. New York: Meridian, 1999.

Night of January 16th. New York: Longmans, Green, 1936; paperback, New York: World Publishing, 1968; New York: New American Library, 1971.

Philosophy: Who Needs It. New York: Bobbs-Merrill, 1982.

The Romantic Manifesto. New York: World Publishing, 1969; paperback, New York: New American Library, 1971

Russian Writings on Hollywood. Marina del Rey, CA: Ayn Rand Institute Press, 1999.

The Virtue of Selfishness. New York: New American Library, 1964. Paperback only.

"The Unconquered." Typewritten play manuscript. Adaptation of *We the Living.* First New York production, Biltmore Theatre, 13 February 1940.

The Voice of Reason: Essays in Objectivist Thought. Ed. Leonard Peikoff. New York: New American Library, 1988.

We the Living. New York: Macmillan, 1936; London: Cassell, 1937; New York: Random House, 1959; paperback, New York: New American Library, 1959.

Newsletters

Bound volumes of these periodicals are available in special editions from Second Renaissance Books.

Rand, Ayn, et al. *The Objectivist Newsletter.* Vols. 1–4. New York: The Objectivist, 1962–1965.

———. *The Objectivist.* Vols. 5–10. New York: The Objectivist, 1966–1971.

——— ——. *The Ayn Rand Letter.* Vols. 1–4. New York: The Ayn Rand Letter, 1971–1976.

Articles, Short Stories, Letters

"Ayn Rand Explains." Letter. *New York Times,* 11 August 1976, 34.

"Ayn Rand Replies to Criticism of Her Film." Letter. *New York Times,* 24 July 1949, sec. 2, p. 4.

Introduction to *Calumet "K,"* by Samuel Merwin and Henry Kitchell Webster. Originally published New York: Macmillan, 1901. Version with Rand introduction reissued Palo Alto, Calif.: Palo Alto Book Service, 1983.

Introduction to *Ninety-Three,* by Victor Hugo, trans. Lowell Bair. New York: Bantam Books, 1962; reissue, Palo Alto, Calif.: Palo Alto Book Service, 1983.

Introduction to *The God of the Machine,* by Isabel Patterson. New York: G. P. Putnam's Sons, 1943; reprint, with Rand's introduction, Caldwell, Idaho: Caxton Printers, 1943; reissue, Palo Alto, Calif.: Palo Alto Book Service, 1983.

Introduction to *The Ominous Parallels,* by Leonard Peikoff. New York: Stein and Day, 1982.

"J.F.K.—High Class Beatnik?" *Human Events* 17, no. 1 (September 1960): 393–94.

"Let Us Alone!" *Yale Political Magazine,* Summer 1964.

"The Money-Making Personality." *Cosmopolitan,* April 1963, 37–41.

"The New Left Represents an Intellectual Vacuum." *New York Times Magazine,* 17 May 1970, 113, 116.

"The Only Path to Tomorrow." *Reader's Digest,* January 1944, 88–90.

"A Screen Guide for Americans." *Plain Talk,* November 1947, 37–42.

"Textbook of Americanism." *Vigil,* 1946.

"Why I Like Stamp Collecting," *Minkus Stamp Journal* 6, no. 2 (1971): 2–5.

Rand, Ayn, Ralph Nader, et al. "Do Our Tax Laws Need a Shake-Up?" *Saturday Review of the Society* 55, no. 43 (November 1972): 45–52.

Secondary Works

Books

Baker, James T. *Ayn Rand.* Boston: Twayne Publishers, 1987.

Branden, Barbara. *The Passion of Ayn Rand.* Garden City, N.Y.: Doubleday, 1986.

Branden, Barbara, and Nathaniel Branden. *Who Is Ayn Rand?* New York: Random House, 1962; New York: Paperback Library, 1964.

Branden, Nathaniel. *Judgment Day.* Boston: Houghton Mifflin, 1989.

———. *My Years with Ayn Rand.* San Francisco: Jossey-Bass Publishers, 1999.

Den Uyl, Douglas J. *"The Fountainhead": An American Novel.* New York: Twayne Publishers, 1999.

Den Uyl, Douglas, and Douglas Rasmussen, eds. *The Philosophic Thought of Ayn Rand.* Chicago: University of Illinois Press, 1984.

Ellis, Albert. *Is Objectivism a Religion?* New York: Lyle Stuart, 1968.

Erickson, Peter. *The Stance of Atlas: An Examination of the Philosophy of Ayn Rand.* Portland, Oreg.: Herakles Press, 1997.

Gladstein, Mimi Reisel. *The Ayn Rand Companion.* Westport, Conn.: Greenwood Press, 1984.

———. *The New Ayn Rand Companion, Revised and Updated.* Westport, Conn.: Greenwood Publishing Group, 1999.

Gladstein, Mimi Reisel, and Chris Matthew Sciabarra, eds. *Feminist Interpretations of Ayn Rand.* University Park: Pennsylvania State University Press, 1999.

Lepanto, Paul. *Return to Reason.* New York: Exposition Press, 1971.

Machan, Tibor. *Ayn Rand.* New York: Peter Lang, 1999.

Merrill, Ronald E. *The Ideas of Ayn Rand.* La Salle, Ill.: Open Court, 1991.

O'Neill, William. *With Charity toward None: An Analysis of Ayn Rand's Philosophy.* New York: Philosophical Library, 1971.

Peikoff, Leonard. *Objectivism: The Philosophy of Ayn Rand.* New York: Dutton, 1991.

Perinn, Vincent L. *Ayn Rand: First Descriptive Bibliography.* Rockville, Md.: Quill and Brush, 1990.

Robbins, John W. *Answer to Ayn Rand: A Critique of the Philosophy of Objectivism.* Washington, D.C.: Mt. Vernon Publishing, 1974.

———. *Without a Prayer: Ayn Rand and the Close of Her System.* Los Alamos, N.Mex.: Trinity Foundation, 1997.

Sciabarra, Chris Matthew. *Ayn Rand: The Russian Radical.* University Park: Pennsylvania State University Press, 1995.

Tuccille, Jerome. *It Usually Begins with Ayn Rand.* New York: Stein and Day, 1972.

Selected Essays, Articles, and Audiocassettes

"Author Wins Royalty Row." *New York Times,* 11 February 1936, 19.

Barnes, Hazel E. "Egoistic Humanism: Ayn Rand's Objectivism." In *An Existentialist Ethics,* 124–49. New York: Alfred A. Knopf, 1967.

Barry, Norman P. "Ayn Rand and Egoism." In *On Classical Liberalism and Libertarianism,* 108–31. New York: St. Martin's Press, 1987.

Bernstein, Andrew. *The Mind as Hero in "Atlas Shrugged."* Audiocassette. Second Renaissance Books. 1994.

Branden, Barbara. "Ayn Rand the Reluctant Feminist." In *Feminist Interpretations of Ayn Rand,* ed. Mimi Reisel Gladstein and Chris Matthew Sciabarra, 25–45. University Park: Pennsylvania State University Press, 1999.

Cox, Stephen. "The Films of Ayn Rand." *Liberty* 1, no. 1 (August 1987): 5–10.

————. "Ayn Rand: Theory versus Creative Life." *Journal of Libertarian Studies* 8, no. 1 (Winter 1986): 19–29.

Deane, Paul. "Ayn Rand's Neurotic Personalities of Our Times." *Revue des Langues Vivantes* 36 (1970): 125–29.

Dowd, Maureen. "Where *Atlas Shrugged* Is Still Read—Forthrightly." *New York Times,* 13 September 1987, E5.

Fletcher, Max E. "Harriet Martineau and Ayn Rand: Economics in the Guise of Fiction." *American Journal of Economics and Sociology* 33, no. 4 (October 1974): 367–79.

Gladstein, Mimi R. "Ayn Rand and Feminism: An Unlikely Alliance." *College English* 39, no. 6 (February 1978): 25–30.

Gladstein, Mimi R., and Robert Webking. "John Galt's Argument for Human Productivity in *Atlas Shrugged.*" *University of Windsor Review* 21, no. 1 (1988): 73–83.

Gordon, Philip. "The Extroflective Hero: A Look at Ayn Rand." *Journal of Popular Culture* 10, no. 4 (Spring 1977): 701–10.

Gramstad, Thomas. "The Female Hero: A Randian-Feminist Synthesis." In *Feminist Interpretations of Ayn Rand,* ed. Mimi Reisel Gladstein and Chris Matthew Sciabarra, 333–62. University Park: Pennsylvania State University Press, 1999.

Greenwood, Robert. "Ayn Rand and the Literary Critics." *Reason,* November 1974, 44–50.

Hardie, Melissa Jane. "Fluff and Granite: Rereading Ayn Rand's Camp Feminist Aesthetics." In *Feminist Interpretations of Ayn Rand,* ed. Mimi Reisel Gladstein and Chris Matthew Sciabarra, 362–89. University Park: Pennsylvania State University Press, 1999.

Hunt, Robert. "Science Fiction for the Age of Inflation: Reading *Atlas Shrugged* in the 1980s." In *Coordinates: Placing Science Fiction and Fantasy, Alternative Series,* ed. George E. Slusser, Eric S. Rabkin, and Robert Scholes, 80–98. Carbondale and Edwardsville: Southern Illinois University Press, 1984.

King, Florence. "Parodic Verses: *Hillarique Shrugged,* after Ayn Rand." *National Review,* 26 September 1994, 61–64.

Machan, Tibor R. "Ayn Rand versus Karl Marx." *International Journal of Social Economics* 21, nos. 2–4 (1994): 54–67.

McCloskey, Susan. *Odysseus, Jesus, and Dagny.* Audiocassette. Principal Source Audio. 1998.

Michalson, Karen. "Who Is Dagny Taggart? The Epic Hero/ine in Diguise." In *Feminist Interpretations of Ayn Rand,* ed. Mimi Reisel Gladstein and Chris Matthew Sciabarra, 199–219.University Park: Pennsylvania State University Press.

Minsaas, Kirsti. *Structure and Meaning in Ayn Rand's Novels.* Audiocassette. Principle Source Audio. 1994.

Oliver, Charles. "Novelist Ayn Rand: How She Became the Most Influential Writer in America." *Investors Business Daily,* 25 June 1998, 1.

Olsten, Stacy. "Something Old, Something New, Something Borrowed, Something (Red, White, and) Blue: Ayn Rand's *Atlas Shrugged* and Objectivist Ideology." In *The Other Fifties: Interrogating American Icons,* ed. Joel Foreman, 288–306. Urbana: University of Illinois Press, 1997.

Overbeek, Ross. "Rand-Bashing: Enough Is Enough." *Liberty* 1, no. 6 (July 1988): 56–58.

Powell, Jim. "Rose Wilder Lane, Isabel Paterson, and Ayn Rand: Three Women Who Inspired the Modern Libertarian Movement." *Freeman* 46, no. 5 (1 May 1996): 322.

Sciabarra, Chris Matthew. "A Renaissance in Rand Scholarship." *Reason Papers,* no. 23 (Fall 1998): 132–59.

Wilson, P. Eddy. "The Fiction of Corporate Scapegoating (Ayn Rand's *Atlas Shrugged*)." *Journal of Business Ethics* (October 1993): 779–84.

Wilt, Judith. "On *Atlas Shrugged*." *College English* 40, no. 3 (November 1978): 333–36.

———. "The Romances of Ayn Rand." In *Feminist Interpretations of Ayn Rand,* ed. Mimi Reisel Gladstein and Chris Matthew Sciabarra, 173–89. University Park: Pennsylvania State University Press, 1999.

Index

The Author

Mimi Reisel Gladstein is the author of three books: *The Ayn Rand Companion, The Indestructible Woman in Faulkner, Hemingway, and Steinbeck,* and *The New Ayn Rand Companion, Revised and Expanded Edition.* She has also coedited, with Chris Matthew Sciabarra, *Feminist Interpretations of Ayn Rand.* Scholarship and teaching in the field of Steinbeck studies have earned her national and international recognition. She was named the John J. and Angeline Pruis Steinbeck Teacher of the decade for 1978–1987 and won the Burkholdt Award for Outstanding Contributions to Steinbeck Studies in 1996. At the University of Texas at El Paso, where she is currently Associate Dean for Liberal Arts, Dr. Gladstein has twice chaired the English Department, been director of Women's Studies twice, directed the Western Cultural Heritage Program, and served as the executive director for the University's Diamond Jubilee celebration.

The General Editor

Robert Lecker is professor of English at McGill University in Montreal. He received his Ph.D. from York University. Professor Lecker is the author of numerous critical studies, including *On the Line* (1982), *Robert Kroetch* (1986), *An Other I* (1988), and *Making It Real: The Canonization of English-Canadian Literature* (1995). He is the editor of the critical journal *Essays on Canadian Writing* and of many collections of critical essays, the most recent of which is *Canadian Canons: Essays in Literary Value* (1991). He is the founding and current general editor of Twayne's Masterwork Studies and the editor of the Twayne World Authors Series on Canadian writers. He is also the general editor of G. K. Hall's Critical Essays on World Literature series.